MILLER'S

SAMPLERS

HOW TO COMPARE & VALUE

STEPHEN & CAROL HUBER

MILLER'S

SAMPLERS

HOW TO COMPARE & VALUE

STEPHEN & CAROL HUBER

Miller's
SAMPLERS
How to Compare & Value

A Miller's-Mitchell Beazley
  book
Published by Octopus
  Publishing Group Ltd.
2-4 Heron Quays
London E14 4JP
UK

Miller's Commissioning
  Editor: Anna Sanderson
Miller's Executive Art Editor:
  Rhonda Fisher
Miller's U.S. Project Manager:
  Joseph Gonzalez

Produced by Deborah DeFord
  & Barbara Marks
Stony Creek, CT 06405
USA

Volume Editor: Deborah
  DeFord
Copy Editor & Indexer:
  Joan Verniero
Proofreader: Fredric Sinclair
Graphic Designer: Barbara
  Marks Graphic Design

The Publishers will be grateful for any information that will assist
them in keeping future editions up to date. While every care has
been taken in the preparation of this book, neither the Authors
nor the Publishers can accept any liability for any consequence
arising from the use thereof, or the information contained
therein. Values shown should be used as a guide only, as sampler
prices vary according to geographical location and demand.

Library of Congress Cataloging-in-Publication Data Applied for
ISBN: 1 84000 541 6

Set in Bembo
Produced by Toppan Printing Co., (HK) Ltd.
Printed and bound in China

Miller's is a registered trademark of Octopus Publishing
Group Ltd.

*On the cover: Sally Pomroy's Marking Sampler, Salem, Massachusetts,
1819; back cover: Anonymous Sampler with Needlepoint, England,
c.1750.*

*This book is dedicated to the
numerous friends we have met and
worked with in assembling their
sampler collections.*

Acknowledgments

Our thanks and appreciation
to the staff of Mitchell Beazley
for producing this volume and,
especially, Joseph Gonzalez,
who kept us motivated and
focused. We are extremely
grateful to Deborah DeFord
and Barbara Marks for their
expert assistance in editing and
designing this book. Our
deep appreciation to Lita
Solis-Cohen for approaching
us with the idea to write this
volume. And our gratitude
and thanks to Betty Ring for
her continued support in all
our efforts.

Contents

▶ Mary L. Hodgson's
Sampler, Salem, MA, 1811.
Silk on green linsey–woolsey.
12¹/₂ in / 31.7cm sq.

An Introduction to Samplers

How to Use this Book

The unique compare-and-contrast format that is the hallmark of this series has been specially designed to help you to identify authentic antique samplers on the American market and assess their value. At the heart of this book is a series of two-page comparison spreads— 62 in all. On each spread, two samplers, related by type or origin, are pictured side by side and carefully analyzed to determine not only the market value of each sampler, but *why* one is more valuable than the other.

Throughout the comparison section, you'll be able to consider the context in which the pieces were created, their intended uses and relative condition, and their importance in today's sampler market. By comparing and analyzing a wide variety of samplers, you'll gain the knowledge and skills you'll need to find and evaluate antique samplers on the market and assess their worth with confidence. The illustrations and call-outs, below and opposite, show how the various elements on a typical two-page comparison spread work.

The book's introductory chapters offer an overview of the sampler market and practical pointers on the care and display of your acquisitions. A fascinating history of samplers in Britain, continental Europe, and America concludes with a magnificent picture gallery of rare and lovely samplers that have appeared on the antiques market.

Finally, at the back of the book, you will find further information on where to see samplers in the United States, other sources of information that may advance your knowledge and understanding of the field, a glossary of needlework terminology, and a detailed index.

The *introduction* presents an overview of the sampler type in context of its time and region, and its place in the sampler market today.

The *featured samplers* include one good example of the type of sampler and one relatively better example.

The *call-outs* highlight each sampler's "value features"—key factors such as material, design, condition, and provenance that account for a sampler's relative market value.

The small *value boxes* (blue for the good piece, pink for the better piece) contain the size and potential value range of the featured sampler.

Pennsylvania House Samplers—1830s and Later

Houses remained a popular sampler subject well into the 1830s and beyond. The format continued to resemble earlier 19th-century samplers, with alphabets covering several lines above a lower section devoted to scenes and decorative motifs—all surrounded by geometric or floral borders. The chief difference as the century progressed came down to the thread used to stitch the designs on the linen. Wool yarn, especially merino wool, became the choice of the day. Consequently, stitches became larger, and often a looser linen ground was employed as background material. The fineness of earlier samplers gave way to more elementary work.

While the teaching of sampler-making continued in every girls' school curriculum in the 1830s and '40s, and the patterns used for samplers did not substantially change, the finished appearance of these pieces did. The bright colors, made possible by the advent of chemical dyes used for wool yarn, made such yarn very attractive to stitchers, with the result that designs and the finished products tended to be much bolder and more colorful. At the same time, due to the larger size of wool yarn, the tiny details of earlier work were necessarily discarded, and the skills required to create such intricate effects lost.

In the collector's market, samplers dating from after 1850 are generally not grouped in the same category as schoolgirl needlework of earlier years. Samplers stitched in wool from the late 1820s through the 1840s, however, can often be attributed to specific schools and are still influenced by earlier sampler traditions. If not from a well-known and highly collected school, these wool-stitched samplers can be excellent buys for a collector. It is important to remember that not all wool-stitched samplers are American in origin; wool thread was popular in England and Scotland far earlier than in the United States.

Magdalene Binkly's Sampler, Pennsylvania, 1834

The bright colors here make the sampler visually appealing.

Thread loss throughout detracts from the piece's value.

Magdalene's inscription line shows damage, probably due to insect infestation, which was typical of samplers stitched with wool thread. Damage of any sort detracts from value.

Interestingly, Magdalene chose to change the border design she used on three sides when she worked the border at the bottom.

Size: 16¼in/41.2cm sq
Value: $1,500–2,000

The *headline* is a descriptive title for each featured sampler, followed by place of origin and an approximate date of creation.

The *captions* offer further specific information about a sampler's design and background.

The *feature box* presents more information on a topic related to samplers.

Nancy Jane Fulton's Sampler, Pennsylvania, 1847

Graphically, this sampler is a visual delight, with a beautifully composed border and landscape and finely detailed elements.

The floral border is particularly well-developed for the period.

Nancy Jane continued a tradition by including the most popular sampler verse in her sampler.

The floral band creates a pleasing transition from the script to the picture portion of the sampler.

Size: 18 x 21in/45.7 x 53.3cm
Value: $14,000–16,000

▶ *Like Mary E. Ford (see page 87) 11 years earlier, Nancy Jane included this popular verse in her sampler of wool and cotton on linen:* Jesus permit thy gracious name to stand,/ As the first effort of a feeble hand:/ And while her fingers oe'r the canvas move,/ Engage her youthful heart to seek thy love:/ With thy dear children let her share a part,/ And write thy name thyself upon her heart. *This sampler is elaborate for its period, with an intricately worked border and bottom pictorial panel.*

◀ *In this wool on linen sampler, Magdalene Binkly stitched several alphabets, numbers, and initials in the top portion of her sampler, then filled in the space below with numerous designs.*

Dyestuffs and Samplers

Until the 19th century, the dyes used for coloring textiles were derived from plants, shells, and insects. All yarn colors—whether in wool, cotton, linen, or silk—came from natural dyes. These dyes were surprisingly bright and colorfast, as is evident in much of the needlework that has come down to us.

Producing textile dyes involved planting, growing, and harvesting the dye sources, and then processing them by soaking, boiling, and straining to extract the dye. The process was tedious and smelly for indigo blue, as strong urine was used to set the dye.

Wool absorbed the dye more easily than did silk. As a result, dyers achieved stronger hues in the wool lots, as compared to the subtler shades of dyed silk. Much of the wool yarn was dyed

at home and used for clothing, crewel embroidery, and household textiles. Sampler makers favored silk thread, which was imported, spun, and dyed, from England and the Far East.

Chemical dyes did not appear until the late 18th century. The earliest of these, "Turkey red," originated in the Far East, then traveled to the Continent, and finally to the United States in 1829. Other chemical dyes followed, and, by the 1850s, aniline dyes became the standard, largely relegating natural dyes to the past.

These dyes produced stronger, deeper colors and shades not found in natural sources. Bright shades of orange and purple in wool yarns are sure signs that chemical, rather than natural dyes, were used.

Pennsylvania House Samplers—1830s and Later   153

Ann Hudson's Sampler with Needlepoint, England

This exquisitely worked sampler has retained both its bright colors and wonderful design.

The border is exceptional, worked in Queen stitch and tent stitch, incorporating various insect, bird, and flower motifs.

The cartouche surrounding the verse is colorful and dynamically sets the verse apart from the surrounding pattern.

Ann exhibits skill with her needle and a great deal of diligence; the ground fabric is tightly woven with a high count per inch, which requires her stitches to be quite small.

The distinctive, combined qualities of this sampler make it far more valuable than the anonymous piece opposite.

Size: 17 x 12in/43 x 30.5cm
Value: $14,000–18,000

▶ *The lengthy text on this superb silk on linen or wool sampler is an exhortation to love, friendship, and remembrance. Ann attributed the piece fully in this way:* . . . This taught by/ Mrs. Watson/ of Bingley/ & wrought by/ Ann H of of/ Huddersfield/ Ann Hudson 1755.

◀ *This colorful sampler of silk and wool on linen incorporates various needlepoint stitches and designs, along with the basic sampler elements of letters and numbers. Needlepoint proved useful for marking or decorating household textiles and clothing.*

◀ *This detailed view of Ann's tent- and Queen-stitch border (from above) shows her range of color, shaded flowers, and geometric designs—frequent elements that appear on household objects and textiles. She may have copied her designs from a popular pattern book of the period.*

English Samplers with Needlepoint   51

Sometimes, the feature box is replaced by either an *additional sampler* or a *detail* that offers a close-up view and further description of one part of a featured sampler.

Understanding the Market

"Knowledge is power," observed English philosopher Francis Bacon more than 300 years ago. Were he to share his wisdom on the subject of today's needlework market, his words might well be, "Knowledge is value." Imagine going to a local shopping mall and trying to sell an $8,000 antique sampler and a $1,000 stereo system, each for $100. The stereo would probably sell, while the sampler went begging. Does that mean the stereo is more valuable than the sampler? Hardly. Try the same experiment at a prestigious antiques show, and people would trample the stereo in their frenzy to buy the sampler. The point is, knowledge drives the antique needlework market. A collector needs to understand the differences among antique samplers. As important, if not more, is understanding the differences among antiques dealers and how reliable a guide each is likely to be.

▶ *Beautifully executed samplers, such as this piece worked in England by Mary Jolley, c.1760, are not uncommon in the sampler market. They are affordable, available, and can be found in excellent condition. Condition and graphic content are the two main criteria in all categories of sampler collecting. Approx. 14 × 10in/35.5 × 25.4cm. $5,000–6,000.*

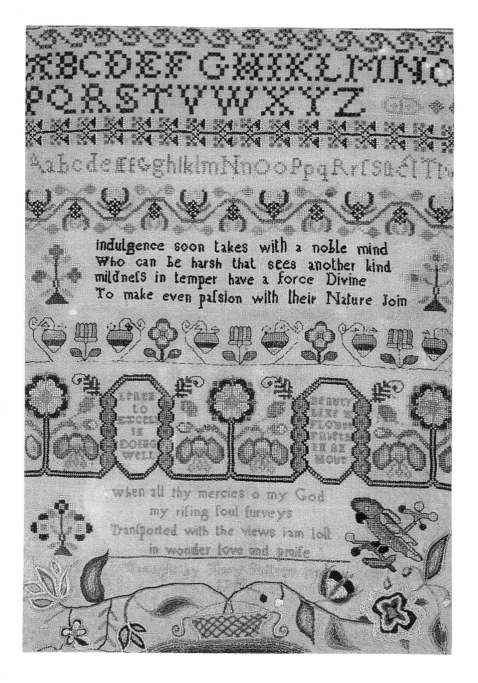

Over the past 25 years, a radical increase in our knowledge about schoolgirl samplers has driven prices up. Added to a few major public and private sales, this increase naturally arouses broader interest, more research, and still higher prices, bringing ever more schoolgirl needlework to the market. A broad-based, consistently growing market over so many years indicates a budding but permanent market, not a collecting fad. For the savvy aspiring collector, participating now—regardless of opportunities one may have missed in the past—makes a lot of sense.

Before the 1960s, samplers rarely sold for more than a few hundred dollars. Behind the scenes, however, a few dedicated people embarked on extensive research of the subject and, in the process, laid the foundation for the future market. By the 1970s, rising interest had begun to push up the prices. At the time, dealers and collectors wondered when a piece of needlework would first sell for more than $10,000. It didn't take long; by the mid 1980s, buyers were routinely paying that much and far more for American needlework. By the late 1980s, a sampler sold for nearly $200,000. Shortly thereafter, a schoolgirl needlework piece (not actually a sampler) sold for nearly $290,000, only to be upstaged one year later by one that sold for about $375,000. Then, in 1996, a needlework

◀ *More detailed and costly than the sampler worked by Mary Jolley, this piece was stitched by Susannah Collins in England in 1801. Her better-developed, visually appealing format, and the intricately worked floral borders and bouquets, all add to the sampler's value. However, English samplers with equal graphic qualities to American samplers are typically assessed at a substantially lower value. Approx. 18 × 12in/45.7 × 30.4cm. $6,000–8,000.*

picture wrought by Hannah Otis sold for $1,300,000. That will probably stand as a record for some time to come. For samplers, the top range at the time of this writing is about $300,000–400,000. Although relatively few samplers sell for over $75,000, the trend is heading in that direction. Far more samplers pass through the hands of dealers, without publicity, than through public auction. The great thing about collecting samplers now is that many wonderful pieces can still be purchased at a starting cost of a few thousand dollars, and such samplers will continue to escalate in value.

Joan Stephens is worth noting here. A knowledgeable collector of textiles and needlework, Stephens's greatest love was samplers and silk embroideries. Her personal collection became one of the most important collections in the United States. She brought together representative pieces from the best known 18th- and 19th-century schoolmistresses who taught needlework.

After Stephens's sudden death in 1996, her collection was offered for sale at Sotheby's in New York. With bidders from around the world, the collection brought an amazing $1,700,000.

▶ *Small, folky marking samplers such as this one, worked by Lucy Griffin Rich in Penfield, NY, are charming and highly collected. Without the three motifs—basket, house, and figure—this sampler would command a fraction of the price. Visual appeal makes it quite desirable. Approx. 14 × 9in / 35.5 × 22.8cm. $2,000–3,000.*

Buying and Selling

It is always wisest to buy fewer but finer examples, no matter what the price range. Samplers worth buying can sell for as little as $500 or as much as $300,000. The most important comparison factor within a price range is physical condition. If two samplers cost the same, choose an easy-to-read or brightly colored sampler over a more elaborate one that is badly faded or stained. Don't try to buy an expensive sampler without: first, a guarantee that it is what it is represented to be; and, second, knowledge of any past cleaning or restoration. Higher prices generate greater temptations among sellers to enhance the looks of samplers; the use of unacceptable techniques may lower the value of a piece or cause irreparable damage. Except in rare cases, the purchaser should also focus on whether he or she enjoys the sampler when it is displayed. Don't rely solely on academic information for intrinsic interest. A sampler must look good to be a good investment.

Selling an antique sampler is not a complicated process if one has the expertise to accurately evaluate the item and understand the market. We have helped hundreds of

◀ *Charlotte Camp stitched her sampler in Connecticut in 1804. With its large bottom panel and floral border, it is far more elaborate than Lucy Griffin Rich's piece (opposite). The trees and figures flanking the house are particularly alluring. In the marketplace, this piece would be worth more than double Lucy's. Approx. 16 × 13in/40.6 × 33cm. $4,000–5,000.*

individuals sell single samplers or entire collections. A seller has several options for help: contacting a knowledgeable antiques dealer or reputable auction house; selling the sampler through an Internet auction such as E-bay; or conducting a private sale. In most cases, the owner wants to sell the sampler for as much as possible, while being fair to the purchaser. The biggest stumbling block for most people is evaluating the sampler. Few people really know the market; consequently, they contact a dealer with skewed concepts of their sampler's value. A well-informed antiques dealer who deals solely in schoolgirl needlework can be an invaluable guide with this first step. There are pros and cons to any course you choose. If you take the time to understand the issues and potential pitfalls, you will be better able to make the best choice for your particular sampler or collection.

A expert sampler dealer often has a good idea of the appropriate market price of a piece. If not, the dealer may do some research, contact another dealer who specializes in samplers, or consult with a reputable auction house. Once the dealer does an evaluation and the owner is comfortable with it, the dealer may offer to buy the sampler or take it on consignment. The owner is likely to realize more profit on consignment. The downside is that no one can predict how long it will take for a dealer to sell a piece. On the other hand, the owner usually has no expense associated with the sale and can get a fair price without risk. A dealer may offer the sampler to private clientele who would ultimately be likely to purchase it, even through auction. In short, this avenue eliminates the costly middlemen. Another advantage of consignment is that the piece remains relatively invisible to the overall

▶ *Elizabeth Moore made her sampler in Burlington County, NJ, in 1826. Her sister stitched an almost identical sampler at the same time and place. The two pieces remain together and are in outstanding condition, worked in a large format. The rarity of a pair of this quality makes them a prize for any collector. 25 ³/₄ × 21¹/₂ in / 65.4 × 54.6cm. $70,000–90,000/pair.*

market, thereby remaining "fresh." This can be an important plus if the dealer fails to sell it, and the owner decides subsequently to put it on auction.

Auctions

Going to auction can be expensive and risky. On the positive side, the sampler may bring much more than is expected. Few samplers, though, sell for extremely high prices at public auction. They usually sell to a dealer. In fact, the sampler may bring much less than expected, and the auction house commissions will be taken from that amount, however small. To guard against ridiculously low selling prices, many auctions allow reserves, meaning that they set a minimum. Unfortunately, even if a piece does not meet the reserve, the seller must often still pay charges associated with the attempted sale. Meanwhile, the item has lost its freshness on the market. Consider as well the fact that whoever purchases an item from auction is actually willing to pay 10–15 percent more for it than the hammer price. The consigner gets the hammer price minus any auction house charges. Usually at least a month—often much longer—passes from the time one consigns an item to auction and the auction itself; and then it usually takes about a month after the auction before the consigner receives payment. The auction remains a good choice for certain samplers, but it carries some potential drawbacks. Read the contract carefully.

Selling a sampler on E-bay or another online auction costs less than a major auction house, but the likelihood of serious competition among capable buyers is greatly diminished. Sampler collectors typically do not monitor online auctions. Furthermore, the seller still must have an accurate idea of what constitutes an appropriate minimum bid, which may once again involve a knowledgeable dealer. Online auctions are usually a great choice for low-end samplers. In such a case, though, a private buyer might be as good or better a choice, especially if one knows the sampler's worth and has a willing buyer.

Selling an antique sampler can be lucrative. Generally, the better the sampler, the easier it is to sell. For additional advice, visit our website: antiquesamplers.com; or contact us via e-mail: hubers@antiquesamplers.com.

◀ *Betsy Fey stitched this wonderful sampler in Fitzwilliam, NH, in 1818— one of several samplers known to have been worked under the instruction of the same schoolmistress. Rendered with silk, chenille, metallic thread, and paper on a white linen ground, it has a market history of selling for $3,000 in 1977, and $65,000 in 1999. Today, its value would exceed that price considerably. 21 × 21¼in / 53.3 × 53.9cm. $80,000–100,000.*

Displaying and Caring for Antique Samplers

A wall can become a window to the past when hung with a sampler or a grouping of samplers. From a distance, these works strike the eye with their graphic appeal. On closer inspection, they call to mind a young girl of 200 years past, meticulously preparing a message for the unknown, distant future: "When this you see remember me," or, "If I could have done it better I would have mended every letter." Displaying and sharing antique samplers—adding warmth and charm to almost any environment—is one of the joys of collecting them. With an inherent respect for the items and a little knowledge of some dos and don'ts, even a novice collector can successfully display and enjoy these lovely pieces while preserving them for future generations.

Samplers that lack graphic punch, or that are predominantly monochromatic, have their greatest impact when hung for close viewing rather than to be seen across the room. The charm of such pieces comes less from their visual appeal than from an academic or emotional response to their verses or other inscriptions. In contrast, samplers that are colorful and graphic can successfully be the focal point of an entire room or area, if they are large enough. A sampler that is visually dynamic but small is best placed on an appropriately small wall or as one piece in a grouping.

Sophisticated samplers were often originally hung as the centerpiece of the most formal room in the house, usually a parlor. Parents, proud of their daughters' accomplishments, wanted to beautify their home while

▸ *Nancy Batten worked her family record in silk on green linsey-woolsey. Measuring 25 7/8 × 19in / 65.7 × 48.2cm, the piece includes names and dates of members of the Batten-Thorp family. It belongs to a small group of samplers worked in Salem, MA, at an unknown school in the early 19th century. The vibrant color and condition, along with a more developed design, make this superior to the sampler opposite. For display purposes, this would far outshine the other.*

encouraging suitors or other visitors to contemplate the family's wealth and culture. The reasons for collecting and displaying antique samplers today are somewhat different, but the pieces continue to add a type of warmth, beauty, and cultural depth to an environment that eclipses that of most, if not all, other forms of antique decorative arts.

Always remember that how and where one displays a sampler can also have a profound effect on the life and beauty of the piece. The most common mistake people make is to hang a sampler in too much light, which causes fading. Other problems can arise with too much humidity, mold that is allowed to grow, or excessive heat, smoke, or other airborne pollutants.

To prevent fading, samplers need to be hung in rooms where the amount of light from any source can be controlled. Most homes have a hallway, stairwell, or room that receives less light than others. In a room that is not occupied during the day, you can always pull down the shades. Even in a bright room, there's often a wall or an area that is protected from direct daylight. Artificial lighting also needs to be considered when you're deciding where to hang a sampler. Fluorescent and halogen lighting

emit more of the highly destructive ultraviolet radiation (UV) than other types of lighting. Some of the newer halogen and fluorescent lighting systems have such built-in correctives as UV filters and/or diffusion lenses. It pays to do a little research if you're considering either type. Keep in mind, though, that fading occurs to a lesser degree from any visible light. By all means, turn on the light to enjoy the samplers, but limit exposure as much as possible.

Protecting samplers from damage also requires attention to moisture. The dampness of the wall and the humidity in the area should be taken into account when considering where to hang samplers. It is of paramount importance to have space between the frame and the wall to allow maximum air circulation behind the frame. This diminishes the possibility of mold growth and is easily accomplished with the stick-on spacers found at any frame shop or hardware store.

Excessive heat is another enemy of antique samplers. Heat accelerates most chemical reactions, and chemical reactions of various sorts are the enemies of fabric. Heat reacts with the dirt contamination in the fabric, as well as with acid that leaches from less-than-ideal mountings.

◀ This silk on linen sampler by Nancy Ring was worked in Salem, MA. Measuring 20⅝ × 17⅝ in / 52.3 × 44.7cm, it contains many of the same elements as that of Nancy Batten (opposite), including the date, 1809. The floral border and sawtooth cartouche are near copies, in fact, strongly suggesting that the girls attended school together. For display purposes, this pair would make a stunning combination if this sampler were in better condition. Hung alone, it would be attractive and eye-catching; displayed in close proximity to a bright and pristine sampler, its staining problems would be more noticeable.

Caring for Samplers

Properly framed samplers require minimal care, when hung in an appropriate environment. Framing protects a sampler from most household dust and dirt. Improperly framed samplers, however, can incur a number of problems. Many pieces were originally nailed or stitched directly to a wood or heavy cardboard backing. The acid in the backing material often causes the background fabric to darken. Exposure to excessive heat or moisture will greatly accelerate this irreversible process. Proper cleaning and mounting, combined with informed attention to a nondamaging environment can arrest such deterioration.

If you are planning to restore or remount a sampler, there are a number of issues to consider first:

Is it in the original frame, and if so, has it ever been removed?

Is it framed in a period and/or appropriate frame that should be reused? Will such a frame be the right size after the sampler is remounted?

If remounting, can or should the finished remounted size be slightly adjusted to fit an existing frame?

Is the sampler worth the effort or expense to remount it? How much will it cost?

How involved is it if I do it myself? Is it necessary to do anything, and if so, is it urgent or can it be put off for months or years? Will the monetary value be affected if it is remounted and framed?

A knowledgeable antiques dealer, museum curator, or auction house can help answer many of these questions. It is wise, however, to understand the steps involved in cleaning and remounting to aid in the decision process.

Antique samplers usually include a combination of different materials, each with its own unique properties. Wet cleaning or the use of any solvents is better left to a professional. Do-it-yourselfers cause far more harm than good when attempting to do anything other than what is outlined below. Major museums are a good source when looking for the best conservators. Many so-called professional conservators have compromised the long-term integrity of the sampler by using harsh chemicals to remove stains, or by simply covering stains with potentially damaging pigments for the purpose of resale or display. Such choices—and the attitude behind them—are inconsistent with the responsibility inherent in collecting antiques to preserve past treasures for the future.

If a sampler is to be stored unframed, it should be lightly vacuumed with a very small, soft brush attached to a variable suction vacuum. A clean screen placed between the sampler and the vacuum is sometimes necessary to prevent the threads from lifting. In some cases, even this step is too aggressive, and a light brushing with a small camel hair lens brush is more appropriate. The goal is to remove as much surface dust and dirt as possible without doing any harm to the stitching or background material. Once dusted, the sampler can be stored flat in an acid-free

▶ *This English sampler, signed by "Hickman," aged 10 years, must have been a striking piece when first stitched in the late 18th or early 19th century. Unfortunately, it demonstrates the problems that can occur when a sampler is not properly cared for. The once white ground linen has badly deteriorated and darkened from years of resting on an acidic backboard. The edges have begun to fray from stress and the color is faded from overexposure to light. Although the damage cannot be reversed, further damage can be stopped with proper conservation techniques.*

box between two pieces of acid-free tissue paper. Anything beyond that should be left to the professionals.

If it is determined that a framed sampler should be remounted, the process generally goes as follows. (This is not intended to be a step-by-step instruction manual, but simply an outline.) The sampler is carefully removed from the existing frame, saving the backboard and any information affixed to the back, such as framing labels or handwritten notes. Then the sampler is vacuumed, and the restorer removes the nails or stitching attaching the sampler to the backboard or stretcher. (*Never* resort to cutting the sampler off its backing.) The restorer may choose to detach the sampler on just one side, usually the bottom, and gently slide a thin piece of museum board between the sampler and its original mounting. This is a minimum-invasion process that helps if preservation of the original mounting is warranted.

To properly mount the sampler, a piece of museum board is cut to the exact size the sampler will be when mounted with slight tension around its perimeter, or to the exact size of the glass if it is going into an existing frame. Samplers are never matted, so the frame's rabbet should slightly overlap the actual sampler. The museum board is then tightly covered with a washed piece of linen or cotton, depending on which best suits the sampler fabric. The sampler is stitched around the perimeter to the covered museum board. The inside of the rabbet is sealed, the glass cleaned, and spacers installed on the backside of the glass. The sampler is now ready to be framed. When completed, the back is covered with acid-free backing paper. It is important to reattach or in some way preserve any labels or information that were originally on the back.

Shipping or Transporting Samplers

When shipping samplers, it is wise to use professional shippers. They have appropriate packing materials and do a good job. If self-shipping, first tape the glass, then place the framed piece in a plastic bag, which protects the frame from scratching and creates a moister barrier. Sandwich the sampler between two pieces of cardboard, then wrap bubble paper around the outside of the cardboard. Place the wrapped piece in a strong cardboard box, preferably one that allows it to be transported upright. Mark the box "Glass" and/or "Fragile" and indicate which side is the top. Ship insured and by the quickest practical method to avoid prolonged bouncing and vibration during travel.

When transporting samplers in a vehicle, allow the samplers to ride upright, as though hanging on the wall, and prevent them from rubbing against one another. Protect them from direct sunlight and extreme heat. If need be, lay the sampler glass side down if it does not have spacers between the glass and the sampler, or glass up if spacers exist. Take security precautions—some samplers are extraordinarily valuable.

◀ *"M. Lisson" worked a most unusual Adam and Eve sampler with two examples of the famous couple. Dated 1836, this English sampler retains excellent color and is in very good condition except for the dark fold marks dividing the sampler in quarters. The piece was most likely not framed when first made, folded, and put away. The background fabric has overall acidic exposure, and the lines have accumulated surface dirt.*

A Sampler Primer

Samplers and needlework pictures are admired and collected today, just as they were when they were first produced. Created by young girls at day and boarding schools, they are the only decorative artwork that were made outside of the home but were not intended to be sold. Designed by talented schoolmistresses and stitched under their watchful eyes, samplers were proudly taken home as proof of a young lady's accomplishment. Today, these beautifully stitched pieces are greatly prized and considered important artifacts in understanding the social environment in which women lived and worked in centuries past.

Until recently, samplers were more or less dismissed as childish endeavors that, beyond their curiosity value, warranted no serious interest. In the antiques world, they attracted little attention, viewed much like the spinning wheel as an example of old-fashioned domesticity. People mistakenly imagined a young girl earnestly stitching by candlelight at her mother's knee. Research has rewarded us, however, with the knowledge that samplers were actually worked at schools—many of them expensive boarding schools—under the tutelage of an instructress. In the last few decades, much of this research has been published, revealing enormous amounts of information about the girls who stitched the work, the teachers who taught them, and the schools and regions in which they were created. Armed with this new knowledge, collectors have looked with heightened respect at samplers and needlework pictures, giving them at last their rightful place as important objects in the field of antique collecting.

Embroidery itself dates to ancient times—usually in the form of decorative embellishments on dress and household textiles—and has perennially provided women with a means of bringing beauty into their homes with needle and thread. The exact date when samplers first became fashionable and were routinely produced remains

▶ *Eliza Coombs's Sampler, Mansfield, MA, 1820. This silk on linen sampler is basically a marking piece, embellished with a strawberry border that is edged on either side by geometric borders and ornamented in the lower corners with additional trees. Eliza worked the five alphabets in different styles and cases. 15 1/2 × 16in/ 39.3 × 40.6cm.*

unknown. By the 14th century, however, depictions of samplers appeared in paintings, and, by the 16th century, many written references to samplers existed. The earliest known dated sampler was worked in 1598 by Jane Bostocke and is now owned by the Victoria and Albert Museum in London.

Samplers as Learning Tools

By the 17th century, samplers became a curricular requirement for learning how to stitch, and most young ladies made them. The samplers were long and narrow, 25–36in (63.5–91.4cm) in length and 6–9in

◀ *Sally Beers's Sampler, New Haven, CT, 1775. Sally made her unusual marking sampler in the form of a hornbook. She stitched her letters on a coarse homespun with silk thread, mounted the finished work on stiff cardboard backed with green linsey-woolsey, and provided a tab for hanging. 11 3/4 × 8 1/4 in / 29.8 × 20.9cm.*

(15.2–22.8cm) across. The girls stitched patterns into their work in crosswise bands, often working from both ends, since the samplers were not intended to be framed but rather rolled and kept in the workbasket as a pattern reference. When a decorative stitch or pattern was needed for trimming costumes or household furnishings, the sampler would be unrolled and a design selection made. This type of work, referred to as a "band" sampler, was made in England, Europe, and the American Colonies.

The earliest known American sampler was made by Loara Standish between 1640 and 1650. English and American samplers are virtually indistinguishable in the 17th century. The colonists retained their British identity and carried British customs and designs with them to their new land. Over time, however, American samplers took on an appearance of their own, becoming less rigid and employing larger motifs. At the same time, they developed regional characteristics, even though most of the embroidery yarns continued to be imported.

The first type of sampler typically attempted by a young girl was a "marking" sampler. The design of a marking sampler incorporated letters and numbers and served the dual purpose of teaching the alphabet and

providing practice for the necessary job of stitching initials and numbers on household linens and clothing. Textiles were extremely expensive and time-consuming to make— they were often noted as the most valuable items in a household inventory. Marking these valuables for identification was an essential housekeeping skill, and girls were taught this at an early age. Although the term "marking" usually refers to samplers that are quite plain, small examples with simple borders or other elements can also fall into this category.

Alphabets obviously played an important part in the design and execution of a sampler, and the letters were worked in many different styles, sizes, and colors—even in the alphabet itself. These very differences often aid in dating pieces; for example, the *j* was not included in the Roman alphabet until about 1800. The *u* was missing at times also, *v* being used for both letters. Girls sometimes substituted *f* for *s* in the middle and end of a word, which indicates that the piece was most likely worked in the 18th or early 19th century. The piece shown below, worked by Julia W. Morse in 1825, is an unusually late example of this. It should serve to remind the collector that such details can only be considered clues, not proofs. The dating of

▶ *Julia W. Morse's Sampler, Essex, MA, 1825. This silk on linen piece is more developed than a marking sampler and includes alphabets, a maker's inscription, and a verse. She developed the borders well and expanded them in the bottom portion to incorporate pots of flowers on green grass, giving the piece a platform and a finished appearance. 16 × 17in/ 40.6 × 43.1cm.*

samplers requires knowledge of time-bound styles, patterns and materials that are typical of certain regions, and designs that fit into a group produced at a particular school or under a specific instructress.

Sally Wales Turner's inscription gives insight into the mindset of a young needleworker in the early 1800s. She stitched: "This needle work of mine doth tell. When I was Young I learned well: Though by my Elders I was taught. Not to spend my time for naught."

Evolving Styles

At the beginning of the 18th century, samplers began to evolve into shorter, wider shapes. Band patterns were replaced in the sampler's lower portion by pictorial panels, with alphabets and verses above them. Borders appeared at this time. These last became quite elaborate over the next 100 years, and, by the middle of the 19th century, borders sometimes comprised a large portion of the needlework.

◀ *Sarah Doubt's Sampler, Boston, MA, 1765. This silk on linen piece represents a group of transitional samplers that were worked in the mid 18th century. Canvaswork pictures were tremendously popular in the Boston area during this time, and samplers such as Sarah's evolved to combine sampler and picture into one needlework. Sarah included a needlework picture, bands, alphabets, verses, and inscriptions. Her bands are typical of the Boston area. 19⁷⁄₈ × 11³⁄₄ in / 50.4 × 29.8cm.*

In the 19th century, family records or genealogies became particularly popular in the United States. In England, girls dutifully copied maps from print sources and transformed them into the main theme for many needlework samplers.

Most background fabric used for sampler work was linen. The English preferred a fine woolen, referred to as bolting or sampler cloth, from the mid 18th century on. In the late 18th and early 19th centuries, the regional background fabric of choice in New England and, to a lesser extent, the mid-Atlantic states, was a green or blue linsey-woolsey (linen warp and wool weft). Embroidery threads came in spun and dyed silk, occasionally linen on early pieces, and cotton on later works. Chemical dyed wool yarn arrived in the 1830s and gradually supplanted silk, and, by the 1840s, was used almost exclusively.

Teachers of Needlework

Perhaps the most intriguing aspect of studying and collecting samplers is the information that can be garnered about the young stitchers' teachers. These schoolmistresses, many of them anonymous and/or long-forgotten, have left behind a stitched legacy that provides evidence of the schooling their female students received as well as the incredible talent of many of the teachers. As more and more samplers come to light, it becomes possible to identify more of the teachers and to pinpoint additional regional characteristics and specific schools.

Schoolmistresses taught to produce an income, whether because they had never married, had been widowed, or simply needed to help supplement family finances. Some of these teachers worked for short periods

▶*Ann Lock's Sampler, Scotland, 1761. This beautifully executed silk on linen sampler carries religious motifs and phrases that were popular choices for sampler designs. The embellished letters are typical of Scottish pieces. Including the name of the instructress, M. Hewart, adds an important feature and can aid with identification of location. Approx. 17 × 14in/43.1 × 35.5cm.*

and consequently left little or no information about themselves behind; others became renowned for the fine needlework their schools produced, and girls traveled long distances to attend and board there.

Female academies and schools came into existence in the late 18th and early 19th centuries. Many girls attended these places of learning, which were large by comparison to earlier country day schools. The curriculum at these schools included a heavy emphasis on needlework skills. It was generally understood that a young woman with talent could marry well and consequently bring more

wealth into her family, and no talent was more highly esteemed than needlework. The schools promoted this concept by emphasizing the importance of exceptional work and design.

Collecting Samplers

Samplers exist in the hundreds of thousands, and it is vital for the new collector to understand that they vary greatly in worth and availability. Simple marking samplers are

◀ *Martha H. Story's Sampler, Hopkinton, NH, August 26, 1826. Martha stitched a large and unusual silk on linen sampler with embellished letters similar to those found on Scottish pieces. The coloring and design have great visual impact and make this an exciting piece. 23¾ × 17¼ in/60.3 × 43.8cm.*

abundant and inexpensive, whereas extremely graphic, colorful, and important pieces are rare and can run to six-figure price tags. The value of a sampler is not dependent on the date or the maker, but rather on graphic appeal, location, and condition.

Collecting samplers is an exciting adventure. Viewing a sampler calls to mind its era, its maker laboring over her work, and her attentive schoolmistress. When the sampler includes a name and date, a little effort often rewards the researcher with additional genealogical information. The design of the work may immediately identify the piece as having been stitched under the tutelage of a particular teacher. And when two identical pieces are dated with the same year, one can accurately suppose that the girls who made them were classmates. Connecting teachers, sampler

makers, their families, and other related information enriches our appreciation of the sampler and deepens our understanding of a shared past.

A new collector should purchase, first and foremost, what attracts him or her, but always with an eye to the visual appeal and condition of the work. It is better to invest in one good piece than to acquire several of lesser quality. Time has proven that the best pieces are the ones that sell most quickly and increase in value most dramatically. Some collectors find a focus for their collection—a sampler from every state or every school, samplers with animals, samplers within a time range, or those with specific names. Whether focused or not, a collection of samplers creates a warm and eye-catching display and provides a beautiful connection to the past.

▶ *Margaret Hitchner's Sampler, Pittsgrove, NJ, June 1840. This colorful wool and silk on linen sampler is typical of pieces worked in the 1840s and later, when the vibrant chemical dyed wool yarns became popular and replaced silk thread. The stitching necessarily became larger because the thread was thicker, which effectively eliminated the fine details of past work. Margaret's sampler is an excellent example from this area with great visual appeal. 20½ × 16⅜ in / 52 × 41.6cm.*

A Gallery of Samplers

The exceptional samplers in this gallery span the years from 1774 to 1840 and represent some of the most visually striking schoolgirl needlework still in existence. All were crafted by young students under the tutelage of creative teachers. The designs of these worthy instructresses have endured to enrich our lives just as they enriched the lives of those first touched by their beauty.

▲ *Rachel Cook's Sampler, Pennsylvania, 1823. On Rachel's sampler, worked when she was 12 years old, the heavily embellished surround and the female figures add to the appeal. Approx. 14 × 18in / 35.5 × 45.7cm.*

▲ *Susannah Wearing's*
Sampler, England, 1833.
This unusual silk on linen
sampler does not relate to a
specific group of samplers.
The applied fabric border is
stitched with an embroidered
floral border in shaded
silk. The interior portrays
a landscape beneath the
verse and maker's inscription.
Approx. 14 × 16in /
35.5 × 40.6cm.

The los of Time is much
The los of Grace is more
The los of Crist is Such
as no man Can re toie
Mary   Coward   1786

▲ *Mary Howard's Sampler,
England, 1786. The top
two sections of Mary's
sampler include traditional
English motifs. The lovely
lower panel depicting a fox
hunt makes this sampler
exceptional. Approx.
24 × 16in / 60.9 × 40.6cm.*

▲ *Mary Ann Coppen's Sampler, Canada, probably Nova Scotia, 1825(6). Canadian samplers such as this are not plentiful and can be difficult to identify. Many were made by American girls whose Tory parents moved to Canada after the Revolution. Mary Ann's work is beautifully designed in excellent colors. 12⅞in/32.7cm sq.*

▲ *Alice Mather's Sampler,*
Norwich, CT, July 8, 1774.
Alice probably attended
school in Norwich and
there stitched this attractive
sampler. The piece's
canvaswork panel recalls
needlework from Boston.
13½ × 11¼ in / 34.2 × 28.5cm.

▲ *Elizabeth Ayer's Sampler,*
Miss Parker's School,
Haverhill, MA, c.1800.
A number of related pieces,
such as this one, were
worked in Haverhill in the
late 18th century. Three list
Miss Parker's School—
one worked by Elizabeth
Plummer, who later became
a teacher and carried on a
similar design. The flowery
borders recall early crewelwork
found on bed hangings
and other household
textiles. 16 1/2 × 20 3/4in/
41.9 × 52.7cm.

▲ *Phebe Lane Moulton's Sampler, Newburyport, MA, 1792. Phebe's work contains many characteristics found in Newburyport samplers of the late 18th century. The trees, flowers, animals, and large vase of flowers set on a hilly ground typify the area, as do the trefoil and heart bands. 23½ × 18¾in / 59.6 × 47.6cm.*

A Gallery of Samplers   **33**

▲ *Mary Cate's Sampler,*
Portsmouth, NH, 1818.
Mary stitched a sophisticated
memorial sampler in shaded
colors that create a dramatic
effect against the green
ground. Memorial samplers
and silk embroideries were
fashionable in the late 18th
and early 19th centuries.
23 × 17in/58.4 × 43.2cm.

May folets innocence &
truth my every action guide and guard
my unexperiencd youth from arrogance
and pride

LYDIA GLADDINGS WORK PROVIDENCE October 1796

▲ *Lydia Gladdings's Sampler,*
Providence, RI, October 1796.
This glorious sampler is one
of a group worked at the Mary
Balch School in the late
18th century. Lydia worked
the layered interior in stacked
rows of verse, house, and
figures. The surrounding
floral border she worked in
an intricate Queen stitch.
12¹⁄₂ × 12⁵⁄₈ in / 31.7 × 32cm.

▲ *Ann M. Martin's Sampler,*
Pittsgrove, Salem County, NJ,
May 1840. Ann's sampler is
an excellent example of the
transition from the early
19th-century samplers to
later work, when designs
became larger, and wool
yarn replaced silk thread.
22½ × 17¾in / 57.1 × 45cm.

▲ *Ann Marsh's Sampler,*
Philadelphia, PA, 1727. Ann
worked this sampler under her
mother's tutelage. An early
date and pristine condition
make it exceptional—and
important because Ann
continued her mother's
teaching. This sampler sold at
auction for a record $300,000.
15 × 11in/38.1 × 27.9cm.

▶ *M.A. Kydet (or R), England, 1819. This most unusual silk on linen pictorial sampler depicts a tale of some sort. The story may have been quite noteworthy for the maker but is unknown to us in the 21st century. The rarity of this one-of-a-kind sampler adds significantly to its value. Approx. 18 × 14in/45.7 × 35.5cm.*

British & European Samplers

English 17th-Century Spot Samplers

Spot samplers are some of the earliest surviving examples of this form of needlework as we know it. (The earliest known, dated sampler was worked in 1598.) The spot sampler recorded patterns and served as a reference, or pattern book, for stitchers choosing decorations to adorn bags, costumes, or household textiles.

Most spot patterns were small geometric designs or renderings of natural motifs—many of them based on textiles from the Middle East. Elements were randomly scattered over the linen ground, and worked in various stitches in silk, gold, silver, and metallic threads that would show the maker's needle skills. The vast differences among known spot samplers suggest that, while patterns were probably swapped among the young needleworkers, the girls often included numerous personal touches as well.

The spot sampler reached the height of its popularity at the beginning of the 17th century. When bands were introduced to the spot work, the sampler gained length and complexity. By the mid 1600s, the band sampler had become the prominent needlework of the day.

Because of their rarity, spot samplers and spot and band combinations are highly prized. They form the foundation and link to the samplers most often collected today. Carryover geometric patterns can be found in borders and bands well into the 18th century. Interest in 17th-century needlework has grown tremendously over the last few years, largely due to research, publications, seminars, lectures, and museum exhibitions. Consequently, prices for good examples have escalated quickly. Good examples can bring several thousands of dollars.

Anonymous Spot Sampler, England, c.1700–1725

The sampler has great graphic appeal with spots nicely balanced.

The central flower creates a heading at the top of the piece that is surrounded by other floral designs.

The variety of stitches used helps to demonstrate the maker's skill with the needle.

Both color and condition are excellent on this piece, giving it optimum value.

Size: 17½ x 8in/
44.4 x 20.3cm
Value: $5,000–6,000

◀ *Stitched sometime during the first quarter of the 17th century, this sampler in silk and metallic thread on linen displays a variety of designs, with many worked in Queen stitch. Diamond patterns as seen here were extremely popular.*

Anonymous Spot and Band Sampler, probably England, *c.*1750

The alphabet is included in typical sampler fashion; it was not always stitched on spot samplers.

Spots and floral elements are carryovers from earlier spot samplers.

The condition is considered good, allowing for the few small thread breaks, not uncommon in a piece of this age.

The color is excellent and the piece quite rare.

Whitework bands of needle lace, cut work, and raised work demonstrate expert skill.

Size: 34½ x 7in/
87.6 x 17.8cm
Value: $8,000–10,000

▶ *This unusual silk on linen sampler with whitework panels contains all the elements found on early 17th-century samplers— alphabet, spot motifs, band patterns, and whitework.*

▲ *This detail from the sampler opposite illustrates some of the variety the needleworker included, both in type of stitch and in design. Such visual interest adds value to any sampler.*

▲ *The unique column design from the sampler shown on this page is worked in a double running stitch and is reversible—the back looks identical to the front. The design may have been intended as a border to be worked on cushions or cuffs.*

English 17th-Century Band Samplers

Sampler making was well-established in England at the beginning of the 17th century. During this period, 16th-century spot samplers were superceded and made obsolete by 17th-century band samplers, and the tradition of sampler making by schoolgirls under a school mistress's tutelage became standard. The band sampler would serve as a useful reference for the young needleworker and demonstrate her developing skill.

Band samplers were worked on plain linen, the length of which was determined by both the width of the loom (24–36in/61–91.4cm) and the sampler width (6–9in/15.2–22.8cm). If the entire length was not worked, the needleworker would cut and hem the fabric. The stitchers were young schoolgirls, usually between the ages of seven and 12, children of middle to upper class parents or guardians. The girls worked their bands in polychrome silk threads, using repetitive geometric designs, floral crenellated bands, pictorial patterns, human figures dubbed "boxers," animals, alphabets, and sometimes a signature and date.

Most band samplers were worked in England, Germany, and Holland. A few can be documented as American, the earliest being that stitched by Loara Standish between 1640 and 1650. The daughter of Myles and Barbara Standish of Plymouth, MA, fame, Loara died sometime between the ages of 16 and 20.

Band samplers are beautiful, intricate works of art. The early dates and exquisite needlework make them highly prized by collectors. Elaborate pieces embellished with figures and metallic threads can bring tens of thousands of dollars. Less ornate, but equally beautiful pieces in good condition, can still be found for less than $10,000.

Gartrud Bond's Band Sampler, England, 1676

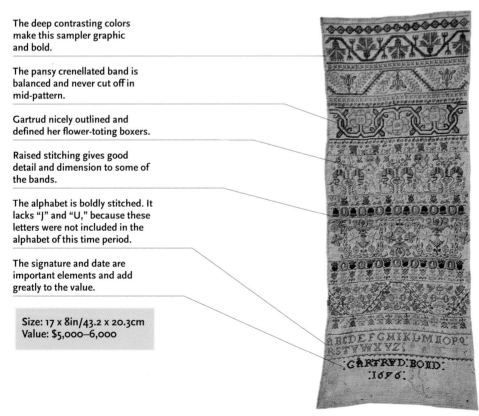

The deep contrasting colors make this sampler graphic and bold.

The pansy crenellated band is balanced and never cut off in mid-pattern.

Gartrud nicely outlined and defined her flower-toting boxers.

Raised stitching gives good detail and dimension to some of the bands.

The alphabet is boldly stitched. It lacks "J" and "U," because these letters were not included in the alphabet of this time period.

The signature and date are important elements and add greatly to the value.

Size: 17 x 8in/43.2 x 20.3cm
Value: $5,000–6,000

Elizabeth Strong's Band Sampler, England, *c*.1660

Beautiful crenellated floral bands provide good focal points for this work.

The soft color palette indicates that the sampler was made sometime after 1650.

The figures appear upside down, because samplers of this period were worked from both directions, and not intended to be framed.

The boxers are clothed and faces, fully embroidered.

Elizabeth Strong signed her name, a value plus.

Size: 36 x 8in/91.4 x 20.3cm
Value: $9,000–11,000

▶ *Large, tall design elements make this a visually attractive silk on linen sampler. The bold flower motifs are also found on American samplers of later dates.*

◀ *Gartrud used strong colors and bold designs for her silk on linen sampler. It is exquisitely stitched and makes a vivid visual impact.*

▲ *This detail shows one of the boxers on Elizabeth Strong's sampler (this page). Boxers were a popular motif throughout the 17th and well into the 18th century. Those who have studied these figures have described them variously as putti of Renaissance design, cupids of Greek origin, or lovers exchanging gifts, as illustrated in a Venetian publication of 1570. Whatever their origin, they were copied in many forms, and usually appear sideways with faces forward and gifts or trophies in their hands. Earlier boxers were unclothed, while later characters became quite stylish.*

English 17th-Century Band Samplers with Whitework

Whitework is a more difficult and complicated form of needlework band than many of the traditional styles. It appears on 17th-century samplers, often in combination with polychrome bands. A young needleworker attempted whitework only after she had mastered the band sampler and shown general proficiency in needlework.

Whitework began in the 16th century in the form of needle lace. Over time, it evolved into more and varied forms, always worked with linen thread on linen and creating a light and dramatic finished piece. The size and shape of whitework samplers tended to be similar to the band samplers, with the same format of rows and repeat patterns. The designs consisted of floral, geometric, or figural elements.

If the materials and themes in whitework were of a kind with the traditional band samplers, the techniques were not. At the time that these samplers were made, lacework was at the height of its popularity in England. Sampler makers used pulled thread work, counted satin stitch, cutwork, drawnwork, and needle lace to create various whitework effects. In some instances, a needleworker would cut a piece of the linen out of the ground fabric and insert a piece that had been worked separately. This took considerable skill and patience.

Whitework has been little understood in the United States until recent research on 17th-century samplers. Far fewer examples of whitework band samplers exist than of traditional band samplers. Good examples are therefore hard to find and highly prized.

Anonymous Band and Whitework Sampler, England, c. 1650–1670

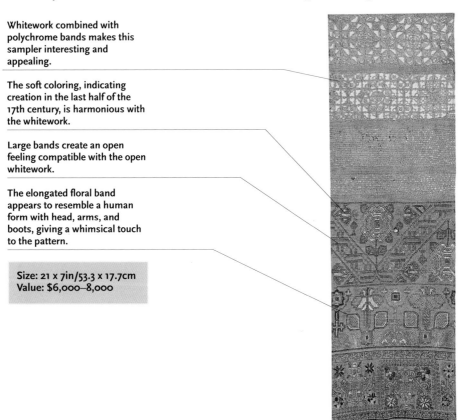

Whitework combined with polychrome bands makes this sampler interesting and appealing.

The soft coloring, indicating creation in the last half of the 17th century, is harmonious with the whitework.

Large bands create an open feeling compatible with the open whitework.

The elongated floral band appears to resemble a human form with head, arms, and boots, giving a whimsical touch to the pattern.

Size: 21 x 7in/53.3 x 17.7cm
Value: $6,000–8,000

Sara Coppin's Band and Whitework Sampler, England, 1662

Beautifully stitched in minute detail, this sampler is well-balanced and attractive.

Detached buttonhole stitching and raised work reveal the creator to be an accomplished stitcher.

The soft colors throughout complement the whitework in the top portion of the sampler.

Note the boxers' interesting clothing and the surrounding large floral pots.

Both the large crenellated floral panel and the spotted deer provide visual relief from the tighter bands above and below.

Sara Coppin's name and date are clearly visible, making this sampler quite desirable.

Size: 34¹/₂ x 7¹/₈in/
87.6 x 18.1cm
Value: $10,000–12,000

▶ *Sarah worked a band of antlered deer and floral motifs on her silk and linen on linen sampler. Bestiaries from the 17th century and earlier inspired many of the animal motifs on samplers in the 17th and 18th centuries.*

◀ *The bands on this silk on linen work are very distinctive, large, and bold. Because the needleworker separated the bands by horizontal lines, they are easily distinguished one from another.*

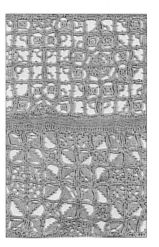

▲ *This detail shows the way lace was worked on the sampler on the opposite page. Lacework of all kinds was in demand in the 17th century; elegant costumes consumed yards of fine lace for ruffs and cuffs. This passion showed itself in the drawnwork, cutwork, and needlepoint lace tediously worked on samplers of the era—techniques meant in part to show the maker's skill with a needle. England's love of lace was so intense that even in the Commonwealth era, when lace was frowned upon, people often smuggled it into the country from France and the Continent.*

English 17th- and 18th-Century Band Samplers

The popularity of the band sampler originating in the late 1500s continued into the 18th century. Samplers were long and narrow—as long as the loom's width or cut to be shorter. Band designs all had their roots in the Middle East, but needleworkers varied and developed their work to suit their personal preferences and linen. When regional differences appeared, samplers made on the Continent took on an appearance different from those made in England. The few existing American examples closely resemble those of England.

A small group of ten samplers from the late 17th and early 18th century have been identified as having been made under the tutelage of Judith Hayle from Ipswich,

England. Dating from 1691 to 1704, these bear her name or initials along with those of the maker. Each example is unique, but all contain similarities, such as the cartouche design that bears the maker's initials. A square design with inner border and corner curlicues, it may replicate a pincushion design of the period. Three other samplers bearing the same cartouche carry the initials of Judith's daughter (RT), suggesting that she also taught.

The band sampler tradition continued into the first quarter of the 18th century, but as the century progressed, the samplers became shorter and wider. Even so, the strong early influence of patterned and geometric bands remained a part of the later designs.

Anonymous Unfinished Band Sampler, England, c.1660–1680

The tightly stitched polychrome bands reveal that the maker was an expert student of needlework.

The touch of red thread in the center gives an interesting effect; it may also indicate that the maker lacked funds for the most expensive dyed silk.

The crenellated pansy panel is one of the most popular and pleasing designs.

An unfinished panel at the bottom gives insight into the method in which the bands were created; it does not affect the value.

Size: 29 x 6¼ in/
73.6 x 15.4cm
Value: $8,000–10,000

▶ *This silk on linen sampler is unusually narrow and contains numerous bands worked in very fine stitching. In the context of the monochromatic color scheme, the red silk highlights seem somewhat abrasive.*

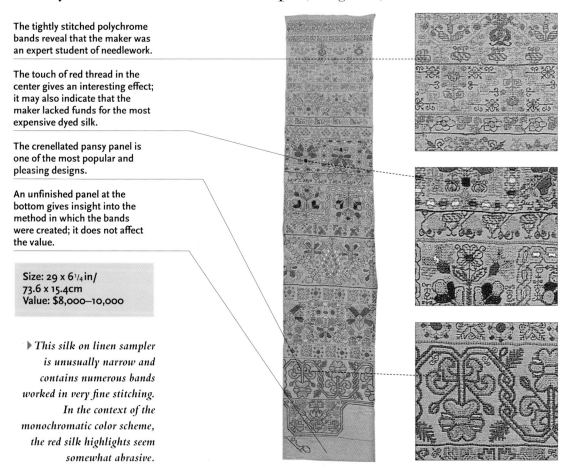

Anonymous Band Sampler, possibly England, 1732

This rare and unusual sampler was worked in an early format, but carries a late date, exhibiting the 17th-century influence on 18th-century samplers.

The coarse linen raises provenance questions, as it is typical of samplers made in the Colonies at this time.

The spotted deer as seen here is found on several of the samplers made under the tutelage of Judith Hayle.

The central cartouche resembles those of samplers from the Judith Hayle School.

A crenellated floral band relates to samplers made a century earlier.

A rare sampler in excellent condition, this would be highly prized in any collection.

Size: 32½ x 8in/
81.8 x 20.3cm
Value: $18,000–20,000

▶ *This silk on coarse linen sampler is probably English, but may be American. The inscription reads simply:* **I Learnt this Sampler With Mistress Peigas And Finished It The 12 Day of September 1732.**

▲ *The detail, above top, shows the spotted deer from the sampler on this page. The lower detail from the same sampler focuses on an inscription that refers to "Mistress Peigas." Despite the inscription, the overall look of the work and the deer detail strongly suggest a design produced under the instruction of Judith Hayle. The subject of much recent research, Judith Hayle is especially intriguing because little is known about 17th- and early 18th-century teachers. When her husband, John, died in 1685, she was pregnant with their sixth or seventh child. She began teaching to support her family.*

English 18th-Century Band Samplers

By the mid 1720s, band samplers of England had started to evolve in shape, appearing in shorter and more rectangular forms. At the same time, they continued to feature many 17th-century designs and elements. Many of the patterns were passed from one generation to the next, worked as always without the borders that would later become popular. As before, the bands were stitched in polychrome silks and the boxers remained as prominent a feature as ever.

In the early part of the 18th century, sampler makers began to add more lettering, alphabets, verses, signatures, and dates. As the fashions of the time turned to a lighter color palette, so too did the girls' samplers. The boxers appeared decked out in a variety of costumes and continued to hold floral offerings in their hands.

Upon completion of a band sampler, a young girl in the 17th century would have continued her needlework education by stitching a canvaswork picture. While the sampler was rolled and kept in her workbasket, the canvaswork—a pictorial piece of needlework—would be framed and hung. Girls worked these canvas pictures in overall needlepoint and usually based them on biblical, pastoral, or mythological themes. By the 18th century, however, samplers evolved into more graphic works, sometimes combining the original sampler elements and a needlepoint picture in a single exercise.

Sarah Turner's Band Sampler, England, 1720

The overall composition and color on this piece create an appealing sampler.

The boxers in their various costumes lend a folky quality to the sampler; one appears to be dressed as a female with a long skirt, while others are unclothed.

The choice to alternate colors in the lettering is typical of the period.

An 18th-century sampler such as this is easier to find than those of the 17th century, making it highly collectible.

The crenellated band is a carryover from the 17th century.

Size: 13½ x 11in/34.3 x 28cm
Value: $3,500–5,000

Mary Dunn's Band Sampler, England, 1724

Extremely vivid colors make this work visually exciting.

By alternating large and small bands, Mary created both interest and definition. Some bands demonstrate a strong Middle Eastern influence.

Mary's excellent choice of color and design, and her careful workmanship, make this sampler a very desirable piece.

The way the alphabets have been separated on this piece makes it possible to avoid monotonous lettering.

The flower-toting boxers under bowers are well-designed and create an eye-catching panel.

Size: 18½ x 9in/47.9 x 22.8cm
Value: $5,000–7,000

◀ *Eleven-year-old Mary Dunn invoked God's blessings on King and country with this inscription on her silk on linen sampler:* GOD SAVE THE CHURCH OUR KING AND REALM AND SEND US PEACE/ THRO CHRIST OUR LORD AMEN. MARY DUNN WORKED THIS/ SAMPLER IN THE ELEVENTH YEAR OF HER AGE 1724.

◀ *Sarah Turner embroidered the following passage on her silk on linen sampler:* SEPTEMBER THE 2 1720 SARAH TURNER IN THE YEAR/ ANNE TURNER/ JAMES TURNER/ SARAH TURNER IN MY DYE/ PROVERBS 27 1 BOAST NOT THYSELF OF TOMORR/ OWFOR THOU KNOWEST NOT WHAT A DAY MAY BRI/ NG FORTH WILLIAM THOMAS FEAR GOD MT. *William Thomas may have been young Sarah's schoolmaster.*

◀*This detail from Sarah Turner's sampler (opposite) shows the boxer in the blue skirt—a rare female boxer. Both samplers show the 17th-century design influence on 18th-century needlework. The bands resemble earlier designs, with the boxer now dressed and more developed.*

English Samplers with Needlepoint

By the middle of the 18th century, the English sampler had completed its evolution from a long, band reference piece to a smaller rectangular sampler intended for display. Backing fabrics, formerly all linen, now appeared as well in a fine tabby-woven wool. Silk threads were often used in combination with wool crewel yarns, and, on occasion, needleworkers would completely fill in some areas of the background.

Flame stitch and Irish stitch were commonly used for household textiles such as seat covers, cushions, upholstery, bags, and wallets. Not surprisingly, many a young needlewoman first learned these stitches while she worked a sampler. The bright colors that were the order of the day in furnishings and garments carried over to the decoration on samplers as well. Often today, one looks at a piece and admires the attractive muted colors, believing them to be as intense as the original. Looking at the piece from the back, however, presents a very different picture. Soft pinks often started as bright reds or purples; in fact, many of the color combinations might appear garish to a 21st-century eye. But at the time, the bright colors were the vogue, and the samplers understandably incorporated the trend.

Just as floral decoration was a prominent feature in the dress of the day, there was a very definite trend toward floral borders and bands in 18th-century samplers. Botanical and herbal publications were also increasingly available at the time, and sampler makers were able to use them as print sources for their designs.

Because samplers with needlepoint tend to be rare, those that are both in good condition and sewn with bright colors are highly desirable. The quality of design is important, however, and collectors should look for those samplers that have more elements than simply alphabets with single bands of flame stitch.

Anonymous Sampler with Needlepoint, England, *c.* 1750

Geometric designs, such as seen here, were generally used for household furnishings.

Bright, vivid colors make this an exceptionally attractive sampler.

The maker of this sampler practiced different techniques in the eyelet-stitched alphabet and band.

The tent stitch was a common pattern often used for upholstery or wallets.

The condition and color make this sampler very collectible; the lack of name and date, however, reduces its value.

The floral band is very attractive and creative, in colors that echo the upper portions. This adds visual interest and complexity to the overall design of this piece.

Size: 11 x 9in/28 x 22.8cm
Value: $3,000–4,000

Ann Hudson's Sampler with Needlepoint, England, 1755

This exquisitely worked sampler has retained both its bright colors and wonderful design.

The border is exceptional, worked in Queen stitch and tent stitch, incorporating various insect, bird, and flower motifs.

The cartouche surrounding the verse is colorful and dynamically sets the verse apart from the surrounding pattern.

Ann exhibits skill with her needle and a great deal of diligence; the ground fabric is tightly woven with a high count per inch, which requires her stitches to be quite small.

The distinctive, combined qualities of this sampler make it far more valuable than the anonymous piece opposite.

Size: 17 x 12in/43 x 30.5cm
Value: $14,000–18,000

▶ *The lengthy text on this superb silk on linen or wool sampler is an exhortation to love, friendship, and remembrance. Ann attributed the piece fully in this way: . . . This taught by/ Mrs. Watson/ of Bingley/ & wrought by/ Ann H of/ Huddersfield/ Ann Hudson 1755.*

◀ *This colorful sampler of silk and wool on linen incorporates various needlepoint stitches and designs, along with the basic sampler elements of letters and numbers. Needlepoint proved useful for marking or decorating household textiles and clothing.*

◀ *This detailed view of Ann's tent- and Queen-stitch border (from above) shows her range of color, shaded flowers, and geometric designs—frequent elements that appear on household objects and textiles. She may have copied her designs from a popular pattern book of the period.*

English House Samplers

By the mid 19th century, the sampler had evolved into a pictorial needlework that usually incorporated a verse of some sort and the alphabet. Almost every schoolgirl made a sampler as part of her curriculum, both in public and private schools. Students fortunate enough to attend more sophisticated private schools could choose a more advanced course of needlework and continue beyond the basic sampler to stitch more elaborate pieces on linen and silk.

The standard form was rectangular in shape, worked usually on a fine woolen fabric in England, and on linen in the United States. The English palette often tended to be monochromatic and the design motifs tightly stitched and exceptionally precise. Favorite elements included a large house or building, flowers, birds, insects, and the ever-popular Adam and Eve. Verses were often religious, many taken from Isaac Watts's *Songs for Children,* first published in 1720. Other popular choices included moral reminders and words of gratitude.

For many collectors, English samplers from the mid 19th century seem to be a logical first purchase. Not only are such samplers relatively abundant, but a collector can usually obtain them for a reasonable price. In terms of relative value, it's crucial to pay the utmost attention to the condition of the piece. Many of these early examples have small holes in the wool ground fabric due to insect damage. Mold is also common on those pieces that have been subjected to damp conditions and usually cannot be removed. Prices vary greatly, but a good piece often goes for under $3,000.

Ann Maria Oliffe's Sampler, England, 1849

This is a nice sampler, well-designed and neatly stitched.

The cartouche border within the outer border frames the verse attractively.

The overall condition is good, with only slight foxing in the ground fabric. Religious verses such as this make it of less interest to many collectors.

The elements are symmetrically balanced, creating a pleasant presentation.

The two outbuildings of smaller size that flank the central house add to the symmetry.

Size: 17 x 13in/43.2 x 33cm
Value: $2,000–3,000

Naomi Moxham's Sampler, England, 1835

The small motifs of animals, birds, and flowers that fill this sampler present a typically English design.

The deeply arcaded floral border provides good definition and serves to hold all the floating elements together.

The abundance of detail and variety on this piece adds to its value.

The overall condition is good, also increasing the value of the piece.

Angels holding the cartouche are found on many English and Continental samplers. In the United States, this design element appears on some samplers from Philadelphia.

Size: 18 x 15in/45.7 x 38cm
Value: $3,000–4,000

▶ *Creating in silk on wool, Naomi stitched an asymmetrical design but managed to balance the motifs well. The center tree flanked by long-tailed birds, and the house at the bottom, provide strong focal points.*

◀ *The inscription on this silk on wool sampler offers a charming look at one young seamstress's solution to poor planning. She did not leave sufficient space for the entire third line of her verse, so she found a creative way to take care of the problem.*

▶ *The detail of Ann Maria's magnificent three-story house (opposite) shows an unusual doorway, fencing, outbuildings, and dancing squirrels. The third-floor windows are smaller than the others, denoting an attic space.*

English Samplers with Pictorial Panels

Pictorial samplers of the first half of the 19th century are highly desirable for their visual appeal. They usually combine a verse and scene, the whole surrounded by a floral or geometric border. Unfortunately, the names of teachers, schools, or places rarely appear, making samplers of this period that bear such information highly prized.

The pictorial panels are usually quite individualistic in design. The needleworkers typically chose to depict pastoral settings, village scenes, and buildings, both public and domestic. Border designs from this period are sometimes carryovers from the 18th century. The girls most often used silk thread stitched on wool, or sometimes on linen. Bolting cloth—fabric used for sifting flour—became such a common ground fabric for samplers that it came to be referred to as "sampler cloth."

As always in the world of sampler collecting, condition ranks as one of the most important factors in assessing the value of a pictorial sampler. Unfortunately, the wool grounds are highly susceptible to insect damage. Ideally, collectors should concentrate on samplers with good visual appeal that are in good condition.

Elizabeth Tice's Sampler, England, 1812

The overall needlework of the sky, with angels holding crowns, helps to balance the lower portion of the picture.

The maker executed her poem nicely, making it easy to read. Its upbeat message adds to the sampler's appeal.

The slight running of the green colors within the panel and on the left edge adversely affects the price.

The pictorial panel at the bottom is well-composed and offers great graphic interest.

Size: 18 x 16in/45.7 x 40.6cm
Value: $3,000–4,000

▶ *Executed in silk thread on a wool ground, this sampler carries a pious inscription common in sentiment for its day:* On The Works Of The Creation . . . Where'er I cast my wond'ring eyes around,/ The God I seek in ev'ry part is found.

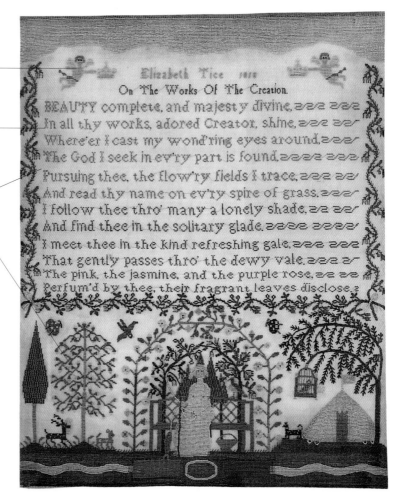

Mary Bourne's Sampler, England, 1828

Samplers of this type are often mistaken for American. However, the church and other elements such as the band pattern typify style and motifs commonly found on English samplers.

Its color, folkiness, and visual appeal make this an excellent example and add to its worth considerably.

The large band border that appears in the center of this piece has its roots in 17th-century designs.

The stick-legged deer and black dog are motifs common to many samplers of this period.

Size: 20 x 16in/
50.8 x 40.6cm
Value: $6,000–8,000

▶ Mary worked her sampler in silk on linen. Her inscription is one of the most used verses: Mary Bourne's Work Aged 12/ Anno Domini 1828/ All you my Friends who now expect/ To see A piece of Work performd/ By me Look on this and do but see/ What care my Parents took of me.

▶ This detail from Elizabeth's sampler (opposite) shows a garden with a woman sitting on a bench under an arbor. She appears to be fishing from a stream with a basket resting at her feet. Note the pet dogs, deer, and chirping caged bird.

English Samplers with Adam and Eve

Of all the designs found on antique samplers, Adam and Eve are the most prevalent and long lasting. From the 16th century to the present, Adam and Eve have continued to capture the hearts and imaginations of sampler makers in Europe and America. Originally, the appeal of these figures was most likely due to their religious significance and the role religion played in the everyday lives of the girls who did the needlework.

Adam and Eve became a standard sampler design—widely copied and stitched in many different variations. While the figures most often face away from one another, examples are occasionally found in which they face one another. The couple are always shown standing on opposite sides of an apple tree with a serpent winding around it. In many early examples stitched in England and America, Adam and Eve are wearing detachable, buttonhole-stitched fig leaves.

Typical of 19th-century English samplers, the sampler makers whose work is presented here placed Adam and Eve in the center, with other bands and motifs around them. Thus, Adam and Eve become the focal point of the sampler, surrounded by various decorative elements.

The strong, ongoing appeal of Adam and Eve samplers makes them very collectible and highly sought after. Fortunately, their similar popularity with the schoolgirls who created the samplers means that they appear in abundance and can readily be obtained.

Mary Appleton's Sampler, England, 1827

Although the sampler has a pleasing format, the staining in its upper left quarter and its monochromatic color scheme greatly diminish its value as a collectible.

Note the geometric band—a nice break—that separates the verse from the pictorial bottom portion of the piece.

The double border, although unusual, lacks the artistic inspiration in color, style, or complexity that would make it an asset otherwise.

The central placement and size of Adam and Eve make them a strong focus for this sampler.

Size: 18 x 15in/45.7 x 38cm
Value: $2,000–3,000

Ellen Eliz. Kiddell's Sampler, England, 1830

The bold vibrant colors in this sampler give it visual strength.

The symmetry is pleasing to the eye and creates appealing balance.

The overall condition and colors on this piece are excellent.

Three large bands of objects allow the viewer to see the individual motifs clearly, adding visual interest.

Kiddell's border of houses on hillocks flanking the cartouche creates a happy effect for the panel.

Size: 19½ x 15in/49.5 x 38cm
Value: $4,000–5,000

▶ *Executed in silk thread on a wool ground, this sampler is inscribed simply with the name of the maker and date of execution:* Ellen Eliz. Kiddell/ December 23, 1830.

◀ *The inscription on this silk on linen sampler reads as a cautionary note:* Now in the best of youthful blood/ Remember your creator god./ Behold the months come hastening on/ When you shall say my joys are gone/ ... Adam and Eve when innocent/ In paradise where placed/ But soon the serpent by his wiles/ This happy pair disgraced.

◀ *This detail of Adam and Eve from Ellen's sampler* (above) *shows her fine work. She identified her Eve with long hair and clad both figures in black sashes. Details such as the snake in contrasting color, the fruit-bearing apple tree, and flying flock of birds add collectible interest.*

British Map Samplers

Toward the end of the 18th century, geography became an important subject in schoolgirl education, and, as a result, map samplers became popular. Most map samplers were worked in the last quarter of the 18th and first half of the 19th century. Only a few are known to have been made earlier in the 18th century. Map samplers usually featured the British Isles, although some focused on towns or counties. Still others depicted other countries, the whole of Europe, or the world. The designs of such pieces were based on available maps. Consequently, even when they appear undated, collectors can date them by the maps they duplicated.

Map samplers were typically stitched with silk or wool thread on a linen ground, or silk thread on a silk or silk satin ground. The latter tend to be more elaborate and skilled pieces. Map samplers featured floral or geometric borders and floral cartouches enclosing the name of the stitcher, her school, teacher, town, and the sampler's date. These embellishments added artistic beauty to an otherwise academic design and gave the pieces a more sampler-like look. Figures representing the four continents sometimes appear in the corners of the borders. While some map samplers are worked in monochromatic colors, others depict counties or countries vividly outlined in polychrome silk or wool.

The map sampler appears to have been more popular in England than the United States. Certainly, many more exist in England. The more colorful linen examples are rarer and in higher demand than those worked in silk on silk. Dated examples are not uncommon.

E.W. Lilly's Map Sampler, England, 1815

In terms of execution, this sampler has merit. Detailed counties of England and Wales are neatly outlined and the surrounding countries and oceans, clearly marked.

Details such as Britannia depicted ruling over the country were copied from a print.

The border surround effectively frames the sampler and keeps the map concise.

The overall condition of this piece is poor—the background silk appears to be glued to the cardboard backing, and the silk has discolored and become foxed.

Size: 20 x 17 3/8 in/
50.8 x 44.1cm
Value: $1,000–1,500

▶ E.W. Lilly stitched this charming example of an oval map sampler, typical of the 19th century. Earlier pieces tended to be rectangular.

Sarah Harris's Map Sampler, England, 1799

English schoolgirl maps were commonly worked in silk on silk, making this piece on a linen ground more unusual.

Note how the counties are brightly outlined and colorful, and the lettering excellent. Major cities of bordering countries are also designated.

Sarah's checked border and compass create a "real" map effect.

The cartouche is very well designed and stitched.

The excellent condition, bright colors, and superbly marked details make this a great collector's choice.

Size: 19 5/8 x 16 1/4 in/
49.8 x 41.2cm
Value: $4,000–5,000

▶ *Sarah worked a crisp sampler with details that successfully imitate a true map. Her silk on linen sampler includes the inscription:* **A/ NEW MAP/ of/ ENGLAND/ and/ WALES/ work'd at Tottenham/ by Sarah Harris/ 1779.**

◀ *This map sampler of Europe is inscribed* **B. Harfield Hammond Court Winchester 1793.** *Stitched in silk on linen, its corners have worked figures depicting Europe, America, Africa, and Asia. In later samplers, the stitched border was often eliminated, keeping only the central oval. 20 1/2 × 19 3/8 in/ 41.2 × 49.2cm.*

British Samplers with Buildings

Few buildings were depicted in the earliest samplers, but by the mid 18th century, needleworkers in ever growing numbers were picturing both domestic and religious buildings in their sampler designs. Chosen from a broad range of styles and time periods, the designs copied structures both from the magnificent British architecture of the period and from buildings described in biblical and mythological stories, which were often fancifully reinterpreted. Perhaps most popular were Solomon's Temple and the grand churches and cathedrals of the day. Needleworkers would most likely have based their designs on images in printed sources.

Building samplers were popular all over the British Isles in the late 18th up to the mid 19th centuries. The buildings sometimes appeared alone on a sampler, surrounded by only a small border; in other instances, they were incorporated into a more typical sampler format with verse and other motifs. Working on linen or wool with silk thread, needleworkers stitched the buildings in counted cross-stitch in the usual sampler fashion. The visual impact of these decorative samplers derives from the prominent position and striking design of the buildings, which were placed in the center of the sampler and sized to catch the eye immediately. These samplers are highly appealing.

Although religious samplers are not as popular with collectors, the samplers with great cathedrals seem to be the exception, probably due to their strong visual appeal. They are not as common as alphabet and verse samplers but are not considered rare. Nice pieces in good condition can be found for reasonable prices.

Caroline Brice's Building Sampler, England, 1836

Although the colors are strong, the background fabric has suffered damage from mildew and darkening that adversely affects the value.

The arcaded border adds complexity and appeal.

The needleworker used large bunches of flowers to balance the building below.

A bold rendition of St. Paul's Cathedral makes this sampler unusually eye-catching.

Size: 16 x 12⅝in/
40.6 x 32.1cm
Value: $2,000–2,500

Elizabeth Booth's Building Sampler, British Isles, 1830

This sampler exhibits a very bold and striking design that is well-executed.

Oversize birds stand as twin lookouts while unrelated motifs drift about on the ground fabric to fill the open spaces.

Excellent condition and coloring make this piece more valuable than Caroline Brice's sampler. Were they in equally good condition, their value would also be equal.

The geometric border works well with the triangular geometric wall.

Size: approx. 14in/
35.6cm sq
Value: $2,500–3,500

▶ *Elizabeth rendered her work in silk on linen, choosing a Bible verse for the inscription as follows:* But will God indeed dwell on the earth/ Behold the heaven and heaven of heavens/ cannot contain thee, how much less this house/ that I have built.

◀ *Caroline's sampler in silk thread on wool offers both strong design and verse. It reads:* Come read my little friend/ And learn this for a truth/ That learning forms the mind/ And manners that of youth.

Notes on Solomon's Temple

Grand buildings were often chosen as the topic of a schoolgirl sampler. In England, Solomon's Temple and St. Paul's Cathedral were two of the most popular subjects.

Construction of Solomon's Temple on Jerusalem's Mount Moriah is thought to have begun in 966 BC. It took seven years to complete and was twice the size of the Tabernacle, the sacred shrine that had long been the center of Hebrew religious life. In 586 BC, King Nebuchadnezzar destroyed the Temple and sent the Jews into exile in Babylon. After 70 years, the Medes and Persians who had conquered Babylon allowed the Jews to return to Jerusalem and rebuild their Temple.

The Second Temple was completed around 515 BC. Jerusalem, however, continued to change hands as Persian rule was replaced by Greek and finally Roman domination. Herod the Great, who ruled under the Romans from about 47 BC to 4 BC, greatly enlarged the Second Temple. But it too would be destroyed in 70 AD.

It is no surprise that young girls who learned this story and were familiar with England's great cathedrals would choose to imagine and depict the ancient building.

English Samplers from the Ackworth School

Almost all samplers were stitched at a day or boarding school. The Ackworth School in York, England, was a boarding school founded by the Quakers in 1779. It was created to educate the children of Quaker families in a protected environment, uninfluenced by the surrounding society.

The school kept its tuition low so that families of little means—as well as those of greater wealth—could send their children for education. The well-to-do constituents were expected to pay more and did, but children from all economic strata were expected to dress and behave in a manner that was plain and neat. Boys and girls received the same instruction in reading and writing, but were then separated so the boys could be given science lessons while the girls were taught needlework and other domestic skills.

Ackworth girls stitched extract samplers—samplers with verses worked on them—and alphabet samplers, the latter executed in bold roman letters. However, two distinctive types of samplers from the Ackworth School deserve special attention: the darning sampler and the medallion sampler. The darning samplers *(see page 64)* were designed to teach mending and weaving skills, while the medallion samplers were more purely decorative in nature.

Medallion samplers are quite graphic and geometric. Recent speculation suggests that the medallions, which are not found in any other Quaker form, were mathematical stitch problems teaching the concept of whole, half, and quarters. Often only half a medallion appears as a form in a border treatment.

Other motifs on the samplers include typical Quaker designs such as a bird on a branch, paired doves, swans, tulips, lily of the valley, and other floral and decorative motifs. The colors usually tend toward the monochromatic and somber. Very dramatic and bold, these pieces are highly sought after by collectors.

Ackworth School Sampler by SP, England, 1806

Its excellent condition and wonderful color make this a very desirable piece.

The many colors that appear on this piece make it most unusual for Ackworth work.

The roman-lettered alphabet is randomly stitched in bright pink.

Note how numbers, letters, and initials are tucked in wherever space permitted.

The needleworker balanced her design with squirrels at two of the corners.

Size: unknown
Value: $10,000–12,000

Sarah Swinborn's Ackworth School Sampler, England, 1802

Monochromatic, large, and grand, this sampler has fabulous visual appeal.

Excellent condition and strong graphic appeal make this one of the major samplers from this school.

Rows of full medallions serve to bring order and balance to an otherwise busy needlework.

The scattered alphabet creates an intriguing game of finding all the letters.

The cartouche indicates that this is intended as a presentation or gift sampler.

Size: approx. 18in/ 45.7cm sq
Value: $15,000–18,000

▶ *Sarah stitched a wide variety of motifs into the overall design of her sampler. No single element or treatment is repeated, making the piece especially intriguing to the viewer.*

◀ *The common ground between these two samplers is the intention to give them away— these are samplers made as presents to another. Note on the sampler opposite that the needleworker included this in her inscription: A/ gift from/ a friend/ 1806 and SP/ to ED.*

The Westtown-Ackworth Connection

One of the best-known schools of the 18th and 19th centuries in the United States was the Westtown School in Chester County, PA. In continuous operation beginning in 1799, it is based on the model of the English Quaker schools. By the close of the first year, it had already achieved outstanding popularity and boasted an enrollment of 200 students, equally divided between boys and girls.

Many of the samplers created at Westtown were identical in design to those of the Ackworth School. This is hardly surprising, given that many of the Westtown teachers had been educated at Ackworth. When these teachers emigrated to Pennsylvania,

they naturally gravitated to the Quaker community and the Quaker schools that resembled the ones at home. At the same time, they taught the designs they had learned as students to the young people who were now under their tutelage. The roman lettering, medallions, marking samplers with cut-corners, extracts, and darning samplers are all designs that originated at the Ackworth School.

Westtown School samplers are not limited to the Ackworth designs. Living in a new land with new influences, the teachers created many variations of their own, including designs that depict the magnificent Westtown School building.

English Darning Samplers

Darning samplers created in the 18th and 19th centuries in Britain, Europe, and the United States are without a doubt some of the most beautiful samplers ever created. The purpose of such samplers was to teach mending on a variety of different fabrics and weaves.

Textiles were among the most valuable possessions in a household, and the women carefully tended and restored them, when necessary. The textiles were commonly passed down from one generation to the next. Mending clearly played a critical role and was considered an extremely important accomplishment.

The English darning sampler probably originated in northern Europe and the Netherlands and was copied in England later in the 18th century. American pieces are few and came primarily from the Westtown School in Chester County, PA *(see page 63)*.

Most darning samplers were executed on white linen in multicolor or white. They were decorated with many small crosses scattered over the ground fabric, usually with a center design or cartouche in which the maker inscribed name and date. Unlike typical cross-stitch pieces, however, darning samplers included patches worked with a needle, in which the thread was woven both lengthwise to achieve a warp and crosswise to achieve a weft. The crossing of the warp and weft created the fabric design being copied. In some cases, a square was cut in the linen and the actual fabric being simulated inserted, with the darning warp and weft threads worked up to the square.

The samplers shown here are quite beautiful, artistically designed, and worked by skilled needleworkers. Because far fewer darning samplers exist than most other types, collectors seek them eagerly.

Matilda Meen's Darning Sampler, England, 1800

Matilda's weaving patches are symmetrically placed and well-balanced, creating a pleasing overall effect.

The floral border and sprigs of flowers relate to one another and are worked in colors that complement the patches.

The overall condition is good, although a little dark staining indicates lines where the piece was folded at one time.

The name, place, and date are important additions that add to the sampler's value in the collectibles market.

Size: approx. 16 x 13in/
40.6 x 33cm
Value: $3,000–4,000

▶ *Matilda's sampler was worked in silk on linen and contains a typical identifying inscription:* **Matilda Meen/ Walsham/ Sepbr 19th 1800**. *She included fewer darning squares than most, but her work is well-executed with good composition.*

Bridget Turner's Darning Sampler, England, 1807

The condition of this piece is good, the design one of the best, and the colors exceptional, all of which substantially increase its value.

The patches are woven designs that are precisely worked.

The meandering floral border lightens the sampler and includes an unusual variety of flowers.

The central basket of flowers is a wonderful, dynamic composition that pulls the eye to the center of the sampler.

Size: approx. 16in/ 40.6cm sq
Value: $6,000–8,000

▶ *Bridget's silk on linen sampler features twelve intricate darning patches. Like the sampler opposite, she included an inscription— Bridget Turner/ 1807— although she neglected place.*

▶ *This detail of darning patches from Bridget's sampler (above) shows examples of pattern darning—a required skill in mending household textiles. The most common weaving types included: tabby, web, twill, and damask. The more complicated required a high degree of skill.*

English Memorial Samplers

Memorial or mourning samplers are unusual and more individualistic than many other types of samplers. Some date to the 18th century, but most were made in the first half of the 19th century. Unlike silk mourning embroideries, which were wholly pictorial, most of the memorial samplers were stitched with a verse and border. The verse could be taken from a published source, such as a hymn or poem, or written personally as a eulogy.

Worked in silk on linen, the memorial sampler was stitched with one color, usually black, or in polychrome silks. The verse was always worked in cross-stitch and the border in either cross-stitch or embroidery. While the emphasis was on the person, design still played an important role.

Memorial needlework became prominent in the late 18th century and continued until about 1830. In the United States, such pieces gained immense popularity after the death of George Washington. Some samplers depict urns or monuments, usually with initials in remembrance of a loved one.

Memorial samplers are much rarer than silk memorials. Because of the personal tone, they are not as highly sought after as other samplers. Collectors of mourning pictures also find memorial samplers of interest. For the most part, these are not the most expensive type of sampler, and good buys can be found. However, as more collectors understand the subject and meaning behind memorial samplers, prices are beginning to escalate.

Elizabeth Ann Smith's Memorial Sampler, England, 1849

Elizabeth created a dramatic presentation in black on white.

The border gives the effect of lace, incorporating black and white blocks within the double rows.

The poem with its redemptive message probably came from a hymn.

The sampler is in good condition. The personal tone and nature of the piece, however, make it less valuable than other types of samplers.

Size: approx. 12in/30.5cm sq
Value: $1,000–2,000

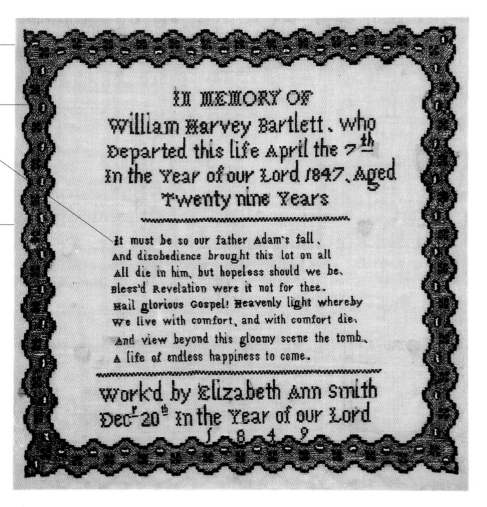

IN MEMORY OF
William Harvey Bartlett, who
Departed this life April the 7th
In the Year of our Lord 1847, Aged
Twenty nine Years

It must be so our father Adam's fall,
And disobedience brought this lot on all
All die in him, but hopeless should we be,
Bless'd Revelation were it not for thee,
Hail glorious Gospel! Heavenly light whereby
We live with comfort, and with comfort die,
And view beyond this gloomy scene the tomb,
A life of endless happiness to come.

work'd by Elizabeth Ann Smith
Dec.r 20th In the Year of our Lord
1849

Eliza Catherine Ann Laxton's Memorial Sampler, England, 1823

Mrs. Mason must have been a rather prominent person in the community to be buried in the Bristol Cathedral.

Good condition and excellent color make this sampler more valuable than the black and white piece opposite.

A large and dramatic floral border frames the long inscription nicely.

The monument at the bottom is flanked by two pots of plants with the name neatly placed between them.

Size: 14 x 13in/35.5 x 33cm
Value: $2,500–3,500

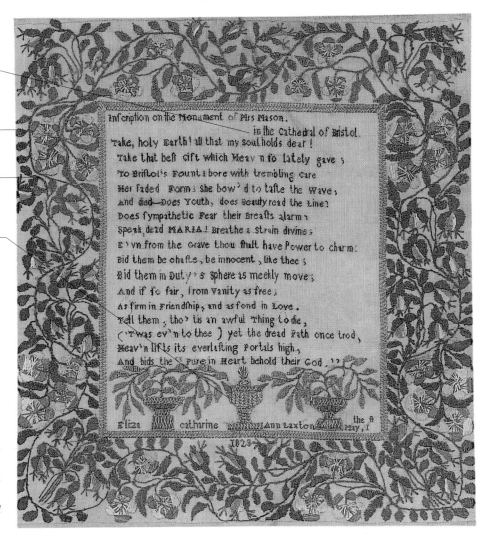

▶ *This sampler was worked in silk on linen and inscribed:* **Eliza Catherine Ann Laxton May the 1st/ 1823,** *followed by a long quotation from the monument of Mrs. Mason in the Cathedral of Bristol.*

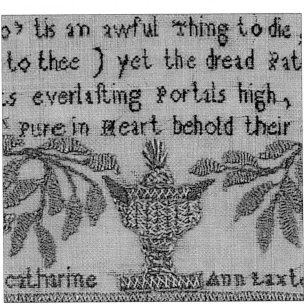

◀ *This silk on linen sampler tells its tale in the inscription: . . . In the Year of our Lord/ 1849 and IN MEMORY OF/ William Harvey Bartlett, who/ Departed this life April the 7th/ In the Year of our Lord 1847, Aged/ Twenty nine Years. Notice that Elizabeth's verse ends on a triumphant note.*

◀ *This detail from the sampler above shows its verse, copied from a monument inscription. It is unusual to find such a quote on a sampler. Note, too, that Eliza has used color, line, and form to great effect.*

Scottish Band and Building Samplers

Scottish band and building samplers have captured the interest of collectors in part because they carry over into the 19th century designs that originated in the 17th century. Usually colorful and filled with numerous motifs, they provide striking examples of needlework as it was taught in Scotland in the late 18th and early 19th centuries.

Typically, this sampler format consists of bands at the top, a cartouche with verse and possibly name and date in the center, and a lower third that is dominated by a large country house and garden. The entire sampler is usually peppered with small motifs of birds, animals, trees, figures, crowns, and other designs. The bands often include a boxer pattern with the boxers either facing the same direction or

facing one another. They are clothed in various ways and hold the customary flower offering.

Other band patterns include floral designs with crenellated piping, or lettering with curly embellishments. All such Scottish samplers are bordered, most commonly with an arcaded strawberry design. Worked in silk threads on a linen ground, needleworkers used a color palette that ranged from soft pale colors, reminiscent of the 17th-century band samplers, to more bold and dynamic hues, similar to those in 19th-century samplers.

Scottish band and building samplers have great appeal and are widely collected. Because far fewer examples exist of Scottish samplers than of their English counterparts, they tend to command higher prices.

Anonymous Band and Building Sampler, Scotland, 1801

Initials worked in pairs are probably those of family members. They are in the typical Scottish style.

The boxer band was executed in strong colors that make it easy to see the boxers distinctly. Notice their boots, an engaging detail.

Although the overall color is excellent, slight running of the pot of flowers into the boxer band detracts from the value of this piece.

The central cartouche is very weak. The color used for the lettering is too close to the background color of the linen, making the lettering almost impossible to read and devaluing the piece in the market.

Size: 17³/₄ x 12¹/₂in/
45 x 31.7cm
Value: $3,000–4,000

Anonymous Band and Building Sampler, Scotland, 1811

The sampler is in excellent condition and has a fine variety of motifs and bands, both features in its favor in terms of aesthetic and value.

The top three bands closely resemble 17th-century bands. The clothed boxers with big shoes proudly present their trophies to flowering plants topped with birds.

The soft colors give a mellow tone, and the overall effect is not too busy, adding value.

The Scottish thistle and camel-like animal bordering the cartouche commonly appear in Scottish designs.

Although the cartouche inscription is difficult to read, it is much stronger than the piece opposite and blends nicely with the overall soft palette.

Size: approx. 16 x 13in/ 40.6 x 33cm
Value: $5,000–6,000

▶ *This young needleworker created a notably fancy house in her silk on linen sampler. A stone structure with slate roof, it has a front portico and fenced garden protected with chains across the entrance.*

◀ *"FW" included many motifs in her silk on linen sampler, including a rather strange pot of flowers to the left of the cartouche. Although she remains anonymous to us, her inscription allows us at least to place her in time:* **FW AGE 14 YRS 1801.**

◀ *This detail from the sampler above highlights one of the popular motifs found on samplers from the British Isles—little dogs with curled up tails. The figures appear randomly and were apparently used as fillers tucked under trees and into landscapes.*

Scottish Lettered Samplers

The most unusual and outstanding characteristic of many of the Scottish samplers is their beautifully embellished letters. Such letters are also found on some German and Dutch pieces, which has led to speculation that the Scottish style may have originated on the Continent. The lettering may consist of the entire alphabet or only portions of it. These samplers often include pairs of initials, identified in some cases as belonging to relatives of the needleworker. The letters themselves are usually thick-stitched with double rows of cross-stitch and embellished with squiggles all around.

Although this lettering provides a quick way to identify Scottish pieces, other characteristics typical of this region also offer clues. Seventeenth-century floral and boxer bands appear on Scottish samplers created well into the 19th century, but rarely appear on English pieces of that period. Kilted soldiers or figures, peacocks, and names with the preface of Mac or Mc all point toward a Scottish origin.

Lustrous silks were often used to stitch Scottish samplers, as were brightly colored wools, especially on later pieces. The background fabrics were linen or wool, similar to those used throughout the British Isles.

Because of the fanciful stitching used in the lettering, these samplers are visually quite appealing and highly collectible. Fewer of them exist than English pieces of the same period, which is not surprising considering Scotland's smaller population base.

Jean Dick Crail's Sampler, Scotland, 1828

The floral band is a 17th-century carryover of a crenellated band pattern.

Lettering such as this is typical on Scottish samplers.

The figures of the kilted soldier and the couple with crowns add visual interest.

Overall, the composition is good, making this a very desirable piece.

A little running of the thread detracts slightly from the value.

Size: approx. 18 x 13in/
45.7 x 33cm
Value: $4,000–5,000

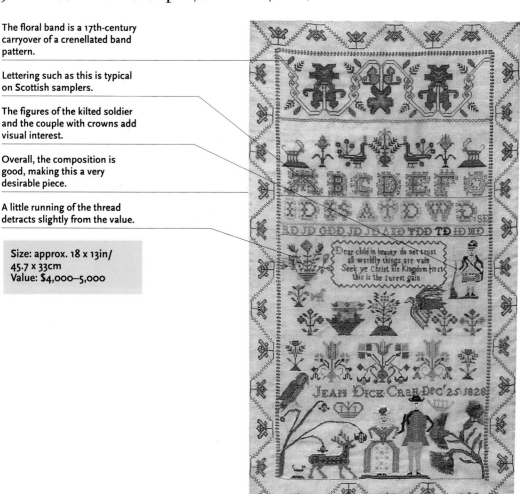

Christian Hutchison Macduff's Sampler, Scotland, 1843

The floral arcaded border frames the sampler well, directing the viewer's focus toward the center of the piece.

The lettering includes both an alphabet in the embellished style and initials in roman style.

A large basket of flowers and two perched peacocks create a pictorial quality.

The design and skill with which this piece was executed make it more desirable than the sampler opposite.

Slight staining in the lower central area detracts only slightly from the sampler's value.

Size: approx. 17 x 14in/
43.2 x 35.5cm
Value: $5,500–6,500

▶ *This beautiful sampler, worked in lustrous silks on linen, exhibits great skill with the needle. This needleworker, like the one who created the sampler opposite, has provided us with a moral lesson in the inscription:* Life's uncertain—Death is sure/ Sin's the wound— And Christ's the cure.

◀ *Floral band, embellished lettering, and Scottish figures add to the appeal of this folky silk on wool sampler. The inscription reads:* JEAN DICK CRAIL Dec' 25 1828, *and,* Dear child in beauty do not trust/ all worldly things are vain/ Seek ye Christ the Kingdom first/ this is the surest gain.

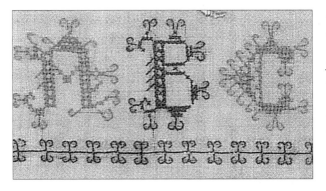

◀ *A detail of Christian's letters shows how beautifully rendered they are, with fashionable, curled tendrils adorning each one. This type of lettering is also found on Dutch and German samplers. In addition to ornamental letters, Scottish samplers may also include simpler letters outlined in a contrasting color.*

British House Samplers

Samplers were stitched by the hundreds of thousands throughout the British Isles and the British colonies. Sometimes a collector can identify a sampler's exact place of origin fairly easily. In other instances, too few examples exist of a particular type of sampler to pinpoint the specific area in which it was made; the best that can be done is to identify it as American, English, or whatever.

One of the most common designs used on samplers of the 18th and 19th centuries is the house. To the sampler makers, the house symbolized security and served as the place to display the finished needlework. Houses depicted on samplers appear in all shapes and sizes—from a small cottage, as on Jean Pollock's sampler shown at right, to large impressive Queen Anne brick buildings, as depicted

in Lydia Haigh's piece below. It's not surprising that beginning collectors almost always want a "little sampler with a house and alphabet."

Stitched houses were depicted in a variety of ways and positions in the sampler design. They might appear as a bottom panel or as a central motif standing by itself. In these cases, the makers often surrounded them with trees, lawn, garden, and animals. Alternatively, stitchers might use the houses as corner blocks.

Whatever the origin and however configured, the house sampler is quite possibly the most collected type of sampler in today's market. Found on the most elementary to the most sophisticated samplers, the house continues as a symbol of home, "where the heart is."

Lydia Haigh's Sampler with Houses, Channel Islands, 1823

The numerous motifs make this a very busy sampler, especially with the monochromatic color scheme.

The large parrot creates visual interest for the top portion.

The flanking houses may represent the school Lydia attended.

The fanciful figures and motifs stitched throughout this sampler were certainly copied from pattern books.

Several similar examples have been identified as being worked in the Channel Islands; this piece thus commands a higher price because of its rarity—one it would not otherwise deserve.

Size: 26 x 17in/66 x 43.2cm
Value: $3,000–4,000

Jean Pollock's House Sampler, British Isles, 1829

The alphabets worked in alternating colors of red and green are often found on British samplers and may help to identify origin.

Although not a fancy sampler, this is still a desirable piece with pleasing images.

The abundant initials most likely refer to Jean's parents, siblings, and grandparents.

Note the bottom panel, in which layered foliage is used to charmingly represent a forest.

Size: approx. 16 x 13in/
41.6 x 33cm
Value: $2,500–3,500

▶ *Part of the appeal of this wool on linen, folky sampler are the warm tones in which Jean chose to work. Her path to the door is particularly inviting.*

◀ *Lydia's unusual shell corners probably indicate that her silk on linen sampler was made in a coastal region. The inscription reads:* Lydia Haigh's/ work/ Aged 10/ 1823, *and,* Be Christ my pattern and my guide/ His image may I bear/ O may I tread his sacred steps/ And his bright glories share.

◀ *This detail shows Jean's rendering of the cabin on her sampler (above). The colorful door and windows create a cozy, inviting feeling. The blue roof gives solidity to the house, which is entirely worked in cross-stitch, leaving no ground fabric uncovered.*

Dutch and German Motif Samplers

Although British and American samplers comprise the bulk of today's collectibles, pieces from other countries are also sought out and included in many collections. Those stitched in the Netherlands and Germany are attractive, well-developed examples of schoolgirl exercises. Many of the early English motifs can be traced back to the Continent and from there to the Middle East, where extensive trade brought many textiles to the homes of Europeans in the 16th century. The designs were later copied in England.

While the connection between samplers made in the Netherlands and those made in Northern Germany is unclear, they share many of the same motifs and formats. Worked in silk on linen, samplers from both regions feature numerous motifs that are religious in nature, drawing on stories and characters from both Old and New Testaments of the Christian Bible. Samplers from both

regions also offer design elements of a domestic sort—houses, furnishings, fences, potted flowers, and such. The floral cartouche held by angels is a feature found on samplers from both regions. Southern German samplers tend to be long and rectangular in shape; those stitched in Northern Germany are horizontal rectangles, similar in size and shape to the Dutch samplers.

Similarities between Northern German and Dutch samplers make identification quite difficult at times. A collector hoping to create a collection solely from one or the other region will want to keep this in mind. However, much research on this group of samplers has been published in the last few years, which has in turn created a very strong market and more knowledgeable buyers. It's worth noting that Spanish and Italian samplers are sometimes confused with German and Dutch samplers, but do not command the same prices.

Sampler by ICH, Northern Germany, 1787

The cartouche, with angels holding a floral wreath, is common to both German and Dutch samplers.

Although asymmetrical, the sizes and placement of the various motifs give a pleasing balance to the sampler.

Note the variety of religious images, including Adam and Eve, Noah's Ark, the Spies of Canaan, and the crucifixion of Christ.

Because of the strong colors, excellent condition, and numerous motifs, this is a valuable example of a Northern German sampler.

Size: 13½ x 17in/34 x 43.2cm
Value: $3,000–4,000

Dutch Sampler worked by TA, Netherlands, 1773

The heavily embellished letters seen here are typical of Dutch samplers and originated in manuscript writings. They can also be found with variations on German and Scottish samplers.

The cradle and *kas* (German cupboard) are found on samplers from both countries.

Many of the geometric designs have their roots in Middle Eastern textile patterns.

This very fanciful sampler is heavily laden with alphabets and motifs. The striking lettering is particularly appealing to collectors, adding to the piece's value.

Size: 16⅝in/42.2cm sq
Value: $4,000–5,000

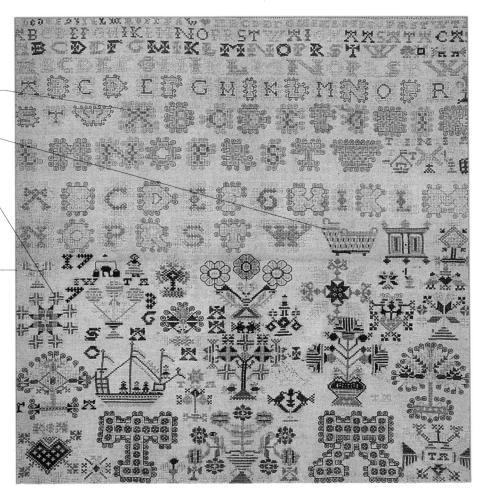

▶ *This beautiful silk on linen example of a Dutch sampler, signed simply T A/ 1773, displays remarkable artistic and stitching skills.*

Motifs from German and Dutch Samplers

Samplers from Germany and the Netherlands abound with allegorical, household, and biblical motifs, many with symbolic meanings. Other floral or geometric designs are simply decor.

One of the most interesting symbolic images is a rendition of Noah's Ark, as depicted on the sampler opposite. The ark appears in the lower left-hand corner as a country house with an owl, a dove, and a stork perched on the roof, and Noah standing in the doorway. The spies of Canaan—Joshua and Caleb—are shown carrying a bunch of grapes in the lower right-hand corner. The ship motif, seen in both of these samplers, is symbolic of the journey to heaven. Other common biblical motifs include the crucifixion and resurrection of Christ, the sacrifice of Isaac, Daniel in the lion's den, and Adam and Eve.

The parrot often symbolizes talkativeness, or female domesticity and marriage. The bee stands for hope and industriousness; deer or stags represent the Greek goddess of the forest, Artemis; dogs represent faithfulness; the lion connotes strength and courage; squirrels stand for mischief; while the mythical unicorn represents power.

◀ *Inscribed ICH/ ANNO/ 1787, this silk on linen piece provides a colorful example of a typical Northern German sampler, containing an abundance of religious and domestic motifs.*

Dutch Darning Samplers

Early household inventories provide ample evidence of the importance of textiles within the home. Linens, bedding, upholstery, clothing, and textile hangings figure among the most expensive items listed in wills and inventories before the 19th century. These were costly goods. They were time-consuming to produce, expensive to purchase, and intended to be used and handed down from one generation to the next. Because of the significance of the textiles, women took good care of them and repaired damage when it occurred. Mending was an essential part of the housewife's duties, one she learned as part of her schoolgirl education and continued for as long as she ran a household.

After mastering the basic needle skills, girls learned darning as a useful and necessary accomplishment. In the Netherlands, darning samplers became an art form early in the 18th century and continued to be a popular form of

needlework throughout the century. The stitcher created a darning patch by inserting a piece of fabric within the linen and duplicating the woven textile with needle and thread. This incorporated the patch into the warp and weft of the original material.

Dutch darning samplers differ from those made in England and the United States. The Dutch format usually consists of large blocks surrounding a central squared block cartouche that contains the name and date of the maker. For the most part, the samplers are borderless, unlike the fancy borders found on English samplers. The Dutch pieces tend to be colorful and often employ more difficult fabrics for duplication.

Darning samplers are both graphic and geometric. These excellent display pieces are collected for their beauty and for the mastery shown by the needleworkers in the reproduction of the darned textile.

Darning Sampler, Netherlands, 1715

Good color and graphic appeal make this visually interesting.

The slight foxing on the linen does not seriously detract from the overall composition.

The early date suggests that some of the fabrics copied in the darning here are most likely from the 17th century.

The tiered and darned cartouche is unusual, as is the floral arrangement.

Size: 13 7/8 x 11 3/4 in/
35.2 x 29.8cm
Value: $4,000–5,000

▶ *This silk on linen sampler provides an excellent example of the intricate work of a very skilled young needlewoman.*

Darning Sampler, Netherlands, 1772

The overall condition and color of this piece are excellent, making it a valuable example.

The squares of darning are uniform and symmetrical.

The white ground fabric around each block separates one block from the other and keeps the sampler's design from looking overcrowded.

Notice how neatly the cartouche has been worked to contain information about the maker and the date.

Size: 19½ x 19in/
49.5 x 48.3cm
Value: $5,000–6,000

▶ *This beautiful silk on linen sampler contains 16 darned examples that are presented in a well-balanced geometric design.*

▶ *These details show the beauty of the darning patches on the samplers illustrated here. The patch at near right, from the sampler opposite, is the work of a more skilled needleworker. Her proficiency is demonstrated by the pattern darning of more intricate weaves. The far-right patch from the 1772 sampler above contains more plain weaving.*

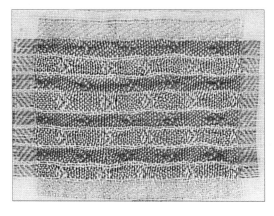

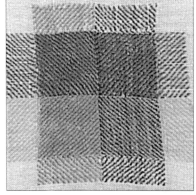

German Motif Samplers

German samplers, with their numerous motifs, are a feast for the eyes. They contain many symbolic designs based on biblical stories and secular life. Early German samplers were made in the band tradition and, as in England, were created as a pattern source that the girls later used for reference in their household needlework. Only as the 18th century progressed did the sampler become an ornamental textile that was actually designed to be framed and hung as a display of an accomplished needlewoman's skill.

Biblical motifs representing both the Old and New Testaments are prominent elements on German samplers and were probably copied to teach religion and stitching simultaneously. Many of these designs can be found on Dutch samplers from both the Netherlands and New York.

Other designs are common everyday motifs, representing village life and customs.

German samplers of the 18th century may include the alphabet in various forms, but verses are not found on these pieces. The cartouches usually include a wreath, shield, or circle that incorporates a floral design and enclosed initials. Generally, names were not spelled out until the 19th century.

Because German samplers are quite graphic and contain many identifiable designs, they are widely collected but command somewhat lower prices than do samplers from England or America. Recent research has aided in identifying the objects depicted on the samplers and their significance. Consequently, these samplers are becoming more popular with collectors.

German Sampler by "FT," 1815

The everyday objects, mixed with biblical motifs and floral designs, can be easily identified.

The darkened ground fabric causes some loss to the value.

The large bowl of fruit creates a strong central focus for this piece.

The initials on either side of the center design probably refer to the needleworker's parents.

The color palette, with extensive use of browns, greens and yellows, detracts from the piece's value.

Size: 26 x 12in/66 x 30.5cm
Value: $4,000–5,000

▶ *This colorful silk on linen sampler, with its many scattered motifs, is a good example of a piece from southern Germany.*

German Sampler by "C.R.F.," 1752

The many bands in the top portion of the sampler include geometric, alphabet, and figural bands.

The figures appear upside down, indicating that the sampler was worked in both directions and probably not intended to be framed.

The large animal motifs—parrot, rooster, dog, stag, peacock, and bull—stand out against the smaller designs representing biblical stories and household goods.

Excellent color and condition make this a very interesting sampler.

Size: 28 x 14in/71.1 x 35.5cm
Value: $5,000–6,000

▲ This detail shows the cupboard from the sampler at right. Typical of southern German samplers, furnishings were often included in a field of spot motifs. The cupboard was often given as a wedding gift and used to house all of the family linens. This cupboard appears either to be made of different woods or painted to simulate inlay. It includes a key below.

▲ Brightly colored with many bands and motifs, this silk on linen piece provides an excellent example of a southern German sampler.

▶ *Anonymous Work,*
probably Newport, RI,
c.1770. This charming
silk on linen piece is a rarity.
No known counterparts
exist. A small piece of linen
used to practice a design
before it was stitched, it gives
insight into how a sampler
may have progressed.
The houses have the
extraordinary detail typical of
Newport, RI, samplers.
15 × 6in / 38.1 × 15.2cm.

North American Samplers: New England

Connecticut House and Figure Samplers

Samplers stitched in Connecticut vary from region to region in style, shape, and format. Wealthy families would often send their daughters to one of the better schools in Hartford, Litchfield, or even Boston or Rhode Island. Samplers from these well-known schools are easily recognized and can be attributed not only to the region but sometimes to the school, and the instructress. For the vast majority of young girls in the 18th and 19th centuries, however, local schools taught by women in the community provided their education and their training in the needle arts.

The designs created by these schoolmistresses were based on the familiar: a sampler they themselves had made at school; a rendition of the school building the girls attended; or elements the teachers drew by hand on the canvas. Consequently, Connecticut samplers include a number of rather elementary pieces, some of which collectors categorize by the name of the town, along with the maker's name and the date.

Houses appear with great frequency in the work of Connecticut sampler makers, while figures appear less often. The vast majority of samplers from this state consist of basic elements such as alphabets, verses, and simple houses and motifs.

The collector can often find a good Connecticut piece at a reasonable price. The graphic motifs dominate the design on more expensive pieces, while simple marking samplers can be had for a few hundred dollars. Buyers should, however, beware of attribution without firm proof. A name and date alone are no guarantee that a simple sampler is from the state represented. Needleworkers did not necessarily depict only their home environs. Keep in mind, as well, that information such as birth date and age must be included to make an attribution complete.

Sally Gorham's Sampler, Connecticut, 1795

Ann Woodruff worked an almost identical sampler to this with the same house and trees, listing the town as Milford—a clue as to this sampler's origin.

The large center-hall house flanked by trees gives this otherwise plain sampler a visual focal point.

Overall toning of the coarse ground linen decreases the value of the piece, but otherwise colors are good.

The strawberry band creates a finished appearance.

Size: 11 x 10in/
27.9 x 25.4cm
Value: $2,000–3,000

Anna Atwater's Sampler, Connecticut, 1773

Tack marks from the original fastening to a backboard can be clearly seen around the edges.

The sampler exhibits a folk art charm, greatly desired by collectors. Good color and composition, as well as the 18th-century date, make this sampler highly desirable.

Large birds such as those seen here frequently appear in samplers from the New Haven, CT, area.

The figures bordered by the letters "A" and "L" possibly represent Anna and her sister, Lydia.

Size: 15 x 10in/
38.1 x 25.4cm
Value: $12,000–15,000

▶ *Bearing the inscription Anna/ Atwater 1773 Aged/ 9 y., this silk on linen sampler is a delightful piece from a young girl highly skilled in needlecraft. The background linen was darned before Anna stitched her piece, demonstrating the value of the linen.*

◀ *This silk on linen sampler bears an inscription that gives both attribution and verse: Sally Gorham's Sampler Wrought October 20, 1795/ in the 14 year of her Age Born December 28. 1781/ Yet fhall thy grave with rising flowers be dreft/ And the green turf lie lightly on thy breaft/ There fhall the morn her earlieft tears beftow/ There the first rofes of the year shall blow.*

The Genealogies of Sally Gorham and Anna Atwater

We're fortunate to know a little about these two sampler makers. A quick look at the known facts gives us a glimpse into life at the time of the samplers' production.

Sally Gorham was born in December 1781. She was the daughter of Samuel and Sarah Lines Gorham, of New Haven, the third child of eight. She married Enoch Ives in December 1800 and died August 19, 1850.

Anna Atwater was born on September 28, 1764, to Jeremiah and Anna Mix Atwater of New Haven. She was the fourth child of eight. The first was a son, Stephen, and the second and third, both girls named Lydia. The first

Lydia died 10 days after her birth on April 4, 1761. The second Lydia arrived on August 9, 1762, and died on September 28, 1763. The four children after Anna were three boys and a girl, named Rebecca Lydia. Anna's mother died on December 23, 1778, after five days of illness. Anna's father remarried twice and died in 1811, at age 77.

Anna married Jeremiah Townsend on June 4, 1784. He was part owner of the brig *Susan*, captured by the British in 1789. Anna and Jeremiah had five girls and three boys; of the eight children, six lived to adulthood. Anna died on August 10, 1852, and her husband, on July 22, 1805.

Norwich Building Samplers

An unidentified building from Norwich, CT, serves as the focal point of a group of samplers dating from the late 18th to the mid 19th century. It may be that this building housed the Norwich school, or it may be some other public building (as was commonly stitched on Providence, RI, samplers from the Mary Balch school). Whatever its function, the building is invariably depicted as a white, center-hall, two-story edifice with three front doors, separated by double windows, and six second-story windows above. The side of the structure appears to have a Palladian window, and the stone foundation is often stitched with a Greek key. The windows usually appear green or blue, and the roof brown, with the corners and doorways outlined in a contrasting color.

Although the needlework may vary from sampler to sampler, the building is always overall stitched, not simply outlined. Earlier examples typically have stitching that fills in either the background over the entire sampler or panels within the piece. The border is often a simple strawberry border, Greek key, or geometric design.

These samplers often feature additional elements. For example, a large eight-pointed flower outlined in brown with white petals and a yellow center may flank the house. Large tulips, hearts, and a variation of the eight-pointed flower usually appear in upper panels. In the 19th-century samplers, the alphabets are located in the center of the piece and typically begin with cursive letters followed by upper and lower case alphabets.

The striking group of Norwich samplers display regional characteristics of style and motif. These were apparently copied as a pattern source and then handed down from one teacher to another.

Anonymous Norwich Sampler, Connecticut, c.1810–20

Overall stitching in the top and bottom panels, as shown here, was common on earlier pieces.

Floral motifs, tulips, and other elements help identify Norwich samplers, adding value.

The building here is identical to the one on the sampler opposite, worked by Amy Crocker.

The staining and slight fading of colors reduce the value of this sampler.

Size: 16in/40.6cm sq
Value: $3,000–4,000

▶ *This silk on linen sampler contains floral motifs often found on Norwich samplers from the 18th century to the mid 19th century.*

Amy Crocker's Sampler, Connecticut, 1844

The curly strawberry border frames the needlework nicely.

Upper and lower bands are well-balanced, creating an appealing effect.

The large, strong motifs are used well and give this piece unusual visual interest.

The overall condition is very good, a plus for value.

Size: 17 x 16in/
43.2 x 40.6cm
Value: $5,500–6,500

▶ *Amy Louisa Crocker was born August 31, 1830, in Waterford Township, New London, CT, the daughter of Nehemiah and Hester Crocker. Such provenance adds value to her silk on linen work in the antiques market.*

◀ *This detail shows the house Amy Crocker stitched on her sampler above. The house is typical of the two-story, three-door buildings found on many samplers from this area.*

Connecticut House Samplers

The house as a central motif on Connecticut samplers continued to be popular well into the 19th century. Usually placed in the center of the lower portion, the house was integrated into a landscape that sometimes included other buildings, such as a church or village, as well as such landscape features as trees and gardens. The house might be the maker's home or school, or a landmark in the area. A variety of architectural details—placement of doors and windows, foundation blocks, and chimneys—often allow for actual identification of the building.

Alphabets became a standard design element. Worked in a variety of types, these elements were separated by linear designs of stitching in different patterns. The maker often included a verse, then enclosed the sampler design with a four-sided border, giving it a finished look.

Although it's often difficult to pinpoint a sampler's origin, a better-attributed sampler in a similar style can help. A related sampler that includes a date and the maker's name and age can help you search records for clues to your sampler's origin. House samplers are very appealing to the novice collector, and they're not scarce.

Julia M. Spencer's Sampler, Connecticut, 1833

Julia stitched the center in a shade close to the ground fabric, making it hard to distinguish.

The zigzag strawberry border is one of the most popular and was used in many variations, both in the United States and England.

The dark overall appearance of the piece detracts from its value, even though the condition is quite good.

The comma in "Spencer,s" is typical of the form used in marking inscriptions on samplers of this period.

Size: 16 x 17in/38.1 x 43.2cm
Value: $3,000–4,000

▶ *Julia's silk on linen sampler includes a house, church, and grove of trees. The shading she used for the lawn areas is unique.*

Mary E. Ford's Sampler, Connecticut, 1836

The inscription verse is the most popular used in both the U.S. and England. The addition of vital dates and location give it impeccable attribution.

The sampler retains good color and has excellent graphic appeal, making it a highly sought after piece.

Mary chose unusual door placement on the right front and side, adding visual interest.

The whimsical flowers and great detail in the bottom panel of this piece add to its charm.

Size: 14 x 12³⁄₈in/
35.6 x 31.4cm
Value: $5,000–6,000

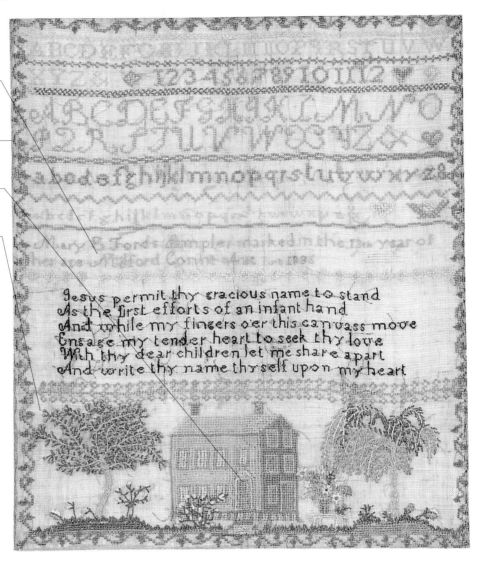

▶ *Mary chose a popular verse for her silk on linen design. It reads:* Jesus permit thy gracious name to stand/ As the first efforts of an infant hand/ And while my fingers o'er this canvass move/ Engage my tender heart to seek thy love/ With thy dear children let me share apart/ And write thy name thyself upon my heart.

▶ *This detail from Mary Ford's sampler (above) highlights the house, whose door placement is peculiar for a dwelling with double chimneys. Such a building would typically have a center door and hallway.*

Maine Floral Samplers

Samplers from Maine vary widely in design, shape, and format. Many of the teachers came from other areas of New England and brought familiar patterns with them. Other designs seem to be particular to Maine and are not found elsewhere. The result is a wonderful combination of light and airy designs, mixed with traditional formats, techniques, and materials.

Flowers and floral designs were used from the beginning of sampler making, so it is not surprising that they show up frequently on Maine pieces. Maine samplers seem to feature floral borders more than any other type, and they frequently display profusions of floral baskets on both alphabet samplers and genealogies. Maine samplers

from Portland can often be identified by their floral border worked in Queen stitch.

Identification of Maine samplers is sometimes difficult, because so few specific groups can be definitely pinpointed. In addition, many of the samplers bear characteristics typical of other locations in New England. Genealogies, of course, are extremely helpful and assure definite attribution.

Maine samplers tend to be attractive, graphic, and often whimsical. They are usually not overpriced and make fine additions to a collection. The most sought-after Maine samplers are those worked in Portland, with pictorial panels and large floral, Queen-stitch borders.

Eliza Fales's Sampler, Maine, 1809

Eliza stitched a large sampler and included decorative designs throughout the alphabet portion.

Thread loss within the verse diminishes the value. Fortunately, the verse remains legible.

Although the last two lines are faded and difficult to read, Eliza's age of 12 years can be detected.

The best element of the sampler is the large, bountiful urn of flowers, which is quite attractively stitched.

Size: 21 x 14in/53.3 x 35.5cm
Value: $3,500–4,500

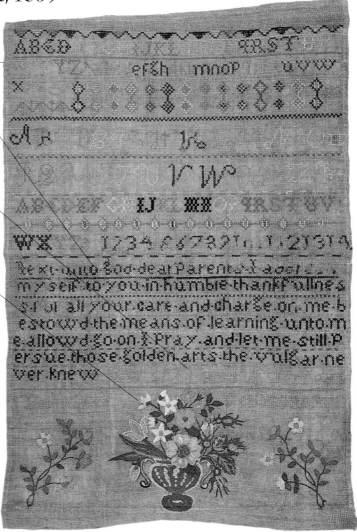

True Family Genealogy Sampler, Maine, c.1827

Crisp and clean with good design and balance, this excellent example features floral design as the prominent decoration.

Slight staining affects the overall appearance a bit but does not significantly detract from the value.

The maker seems to have thought of adding leaves to the bottom corners—pencil marks can still be detected.

The basket with upward leaf design is unusual.

The floral border worked in satin stitch is a typical design on samplers from Maine.

Size: 17 x 15in/43.2 x 38.1cm
Value: $5,000–6,000

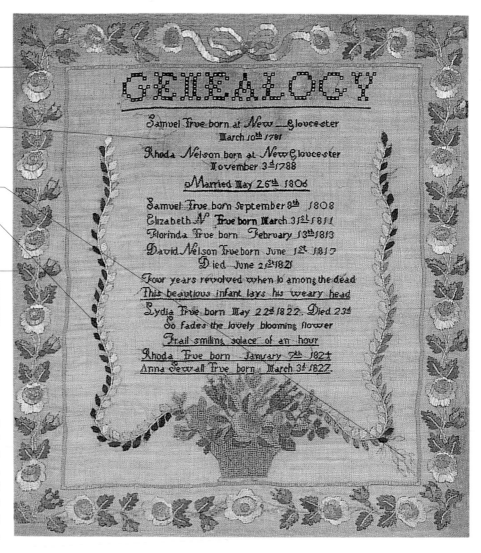

▶ *This lovely genealogy with floral border was probably stitched by either Elizabeth or Florinda. In silk on linen, the piece tells in brief, but with poetry, of one family's typical losses of young family members.*

◀ *Eliza stitched her silk on linen sampler in Thomaston, ME, using a traditional alphabet and verse. Rediscovered in the South, this sampler was once thought to have been stitched in Georgia, which has a town named Thomaston. Research showed, however, that Thomaston, GA, did not exist in 1809. The only known Thomaston at that time was Thomaston, ME. Eliza married Joseph Colson on May 22, 1826, in Thomaston, ME.*

◀ *This detail shows Eliza's elaborate floral bouquet from her sampler (opposite). She carefully outlined stems and flowers and filled them in with contrasting shaded silks. The pot is shaped and decorated with large handles and a pedestal base. Part of the beauty lies in the asymmetry of the arrangement.*

Maine Floral Samplers— Carnation Motif

Although Maine was settled in the 17th century, it was not as heavily populated as some of the other New England states and was burdened with various conflicts until after the Revolutionary War. Most of the Maine samplers existing today date from the late 18th to the mid 19th century and come from the more developed southeast region.

Floral designs appear to have enjoyed the most popularity among Maine needleworkers; some of them are clearly borrowed from other regions, while others are apparently of local invention. One particular floral element that appears frequently on Maine samplers is a squishy little carnation-like flower. This design can also be found on needlework from Massachusetts and New Hampshire dating to the mid 18th century. Both of the samplers shown here include this detail. On some samplers, the carnation appears stemless; on others, it is rounder or straighter. Occasionally it is used in borders. Always, however, it is layered with contrasting colors. It may be a carryover from early English patterns. Other elements in the Maine designs, although not as popular, include geometric boxes and diamonds worked as bands, corners, or fillers.

Often large, the Maine floral samplers are quite graphic, well-presented, and fairly priced. A generously sized sampler can often hang alone on a wall, or it can make a dynamic statement hanging above a piece of furniture. As with samplers from any area, good color and condition, along with visual appeal, constitute the most important factors for the collector.

Christiania Heard's Sampler, Maine, c.1820

Christiania worked four alphabets and an inscription line, but omitted a verse.

Light areas denote paper backing, not staining. The entire border was stitched through both linen ground and paper backing.

The bright, colorful sampler is in excellent condition and contains folky elements that are highly desirable to the collector.

The corner blocks and carnation motif are typical Maine indicators; Christiania's added elements seem to be her own.

Size: 17in/43.2cm sq
Value: $8,000–10,000

▶ *Christiania was born in Sanford, York, ME, the daughter of Jacob and Sarah Hill Heard. Her silk on linen sampler is quite different from Mary's (opposite), but she used the same carnation motif.*

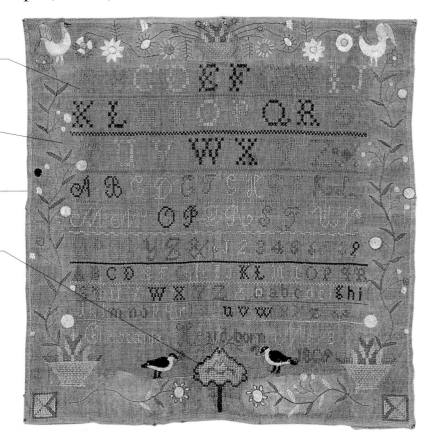

Mary Jane Owen's Sampler, Maine, *c.*1820–30

Mary organized her sampler traditionally, placing her alphabets above the verse and her design elements below.

The four-sided strawberry border, with exterior and interior white diamond bands, makes an attractive design frame.

Multicolored diamonds appear frequently on Maine samplers as fillers or bands worked in Queen, cross, or satin stitch.

Mary's tiered trees are common elements on samplers from the Northeast, especially New Hampshire and Maine.

Size: 28 x 20in/71 x 50.8cm
Value: $6,000–7,000

▶ *Mary's silk on linen sampler fits into a large group of similar samplers from southeast Maine. She stitched the most common verse found on samplers.*

▶ *The carnation-like flowers from the two samplers shown on these pages are found on samplers throughout northeast New England. Some appear as a rounded flower; others look flatter and elongated. They are often worked in two to three different colors, creating the texture within the shape.*

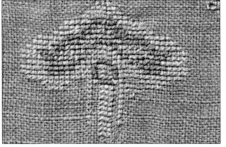

Maine Family Records

Family records and genealogies are personal needlework pieces that list the birth, death, and marriage dates of family members. They offer important historical insights and clues about family life in a specific era. They were particularly popular in Maine, and many remain in existence.

The family register, record, or genealogy, as they are variously called, were worked in a wide variety of patterns and formats in Maine. The easiest to recognize come from Portland, as their distinctive borders provide a solid clue as to origin. The large rose borders with big bowknots surround not only registers, but also the alphabet, verse, and pictorial panels found on Maine samplers. Other family records from Maine were based on designs devised by rural teachers or students, who drew on their own imaginations or reworked images they had seen elsewhere. The two samplers shown here are both bordered with large flowers that bear some resemblance to one another, but their presentations are entirely different.

Registers provide a fascinating view of family life in a bygone age. Historically important, these samplers have been slow to gain in popularity. Among collectors, two opposite reactions seem to prevail: the collectors either love the registers for all they reveal about life in an earlier America, or they shy away from them, because the samplers are too personal and too specific to someone else's family heritage. Several major collections, however, are made up entirely of family registers. Because the demand is not as great for registers, many excellent buys can be found within this group.

Emily Knox's Sampler, Maine, 1826

The content is recorded in traditional fashion—the chief interest lies in the design of the border, which is fanciful, decorative, and colorful.

The large roses are similar to those found on other Maine samplers.

Emily provides, by implication, the information that she was 12 years old when she made this piece.

The pot at bottom looks too small to hold the abundance of flowers, adding to the charm.

Size: approx 17 x 14in/ 43.2 x 35.5cm
Value: $3,000–4,000

▶ *Emily Knox created her register in silk on linen gauze. The sampler was produced in York, ME. Emily lists both her birth date and the date when she stitched the sampler.*

Mary W. Merrill's Sampler, Maine, 1817

Mary's border is typical of Portland pieces, with full roses stitched in pink and white.

The block lettering is graphic, and also common to Portland samplers.

The tombs within black boxes are characteristic of this school and commemorate Mary's sister Lydia and possibly a grandparent or other relative.

Samplers from Portland are highly sought after and can command strong prices.

This piece is in excellent condition with only slight fading.

Size: 20 x 18in/50.8 x 45.7cm
Value: $12,000–18,000

▶ *Mary stitched a very large and complete family genealogy in typical Portland style on her silk on linen sampler. She also included a benediction of sorts:* O RESIGNATION heavenly power/ Our warmest thoughts engage/ Thou art the safest guide of youth/ The fole fupport of age./ Teach us the hand of love divine/ In evils to discern/ Tis the first lesson which we need/ The latest which we learn.

Family Registers

Mary Merrill never knew her firstborn sister Lydia, but 14 years later, she still memorialized her in her sampler. From the Merrill register, we also learn that Martha was 24 and John was 30 when their first child Lydia was born. Mary appeared 30 months later, and shortly after that, Lydia died. The second Lydia—named according to tradition after the daughter who died—arrived 23 months after Mary, followed by John, 34 months later, and twins, 30 months after that. Martha was just 35.

The Knox Record (opposite) reveals that Emily was the youngest of 10 children. Her father and mother —22 and 17, respectively, when they married—had their first child 16 months after their marriage and lost her three months later. The next seven children lived, born at intervals of 16 months, 23 months, 23 months, 17 months, 22 months, 28 months, and 34 months. The ninth child died at 1½ months, and Emily arrived 17 months afterward—ten children in 18 years.

Massachusetts Marking Samplers

Marking samplers are simple needlework samplers that are limited to the alphabet and numbers, sometimes including a name, a date, and/or small decorative motifs. They were usually young girls' first samplers. The word "marking" in marking samplers refers to putting identifying initials on household linens. Linens were expensive commodities at the time of these samplers. They needed to be identified for rotation to extend their life, or to ensure return to the correct household if they were sent out for cleaning or repair. Marking samplers allowed young needleworkers to practice for this crucial chore. They also helped the makers learn the alphabet.

Unlike the more advanced pictorial samplers, marking samplers show very few regional characteristics. This often makes it impossible to identify their origin, unless sufficient information about the maker exists that can lead to accurate genealogical research. Such information typically does not appear on the sampler itself, primarily because marking samplers were usually not made with the expectation that they would be framed.

Because marking samplers appear on the market in great numbers and at relatively modest prices, many collectors make them the subject of an entire collection. When buying a marking sampler, a collector is wise to choose one with no more than slight fading or other damage. Simple marking samplers that have faded to any significant extent or have suffered much thread loss are neither a good investment nor a pleasure to look at.

Martha Longfell's Sampler, Massachusetts, c.1800–20

The background linen here is coarser than the linen on many samplers, making it easier to stitch on it.

Though the sampler lacks color, it has the virtue of being clearly legible.

The overall condition on this piece is good.

The only attribution here is the maker's name, which gives the collector less to go on than in the case of fuller inscriptions.

Size: 6 x 8½in/15.2 x 21.6cm
Value: $300–500

Eleanor Dolbeare's Sampler, Massachusetts, 1795

The decorative bands are somewhat varied in color and type of stitching, a plus for value.

The contrast between the background and stitching makes this sampler easy to read.

Name, age, and date are important assets to this sampler.

The flowering vine adds visual appeal and makes the sampler more desirable to collectors.

Little mistakes, as in the start of the word "sampler," add to the charm of the piece.

Eleanor seems to have fit in the numbers as an afterthought, which in this case adds interest.

> Size: 10 x 7⅝/25.4 x 19.4cm
> Value: $1,200–1,500

▶ *This silk on linen piece is more elaborate than a simple marking sampler but still suffers from being under-embellished. The flowering vine, although rather uninspired, gives the sampler its only hint of whimsy. Eleanor included her name, age, and date, which are invaluable for identifying the origin of her work.*

◀ *This small silk on linen marking sampler is typical of a child's first attempt. The alphabet, numbers, and name are worked on a coarse linen background, separated by lines of stitching. This was plainly intended primarily as a teaching tool for marking household linens, not as a decorative sampler to be framed and displayed.*

◀ *This well-developed marking sampler by Harriet Maria Savory includes a strawberry border, three alphabets worked in different styles, and an apt verse concerning needlework. Harriet was born in Essex, MA, on September 11, 1811, the daughter of Ebenezer and Priscilla Hale Savory. She created this 12 × 10in/ 30.4 × 25.4cm piece in 1822 at age 11.*

Massachusetts Marking Samplers—Varieties

After completing a basic alphabet sampler, a fledgling schoolgirl often graduated to other forms and styles of sampler making. Simple marking pieces were sometimes created as small presentation needlework, designed to be given away or displayed. These pieces were often made for family members or friends to commemorate an event.

Samplers recording a birth—another type of marking sampler—were usually small pieces stating the name of the newborn child and his or her birth date. Worked in the usual silk on linen, such samplers could be made quickly from leftover scraps of material and thread. They could also provide an opportunity for young needleworkers to learn different types of stitches and techniques.

Small decorative floral samplers also enjoyed popularity in Massachusetts. Usually worked by young girls, these pieces often appeared in small sizes that would not overwhelm a novice and could be completed in a short time. The name of the maker, date, and age were often included on these samplers.

There are far fewer small needleworks of this type than larger samplers made in the traditional style. It is possible that many of the small pieces were made at home under the supervision of a mother or older sister. The designs tend to be individualistic and to relate to a specific occasion or time. Eagerly collected because of their rarity, the simpler of these samplers are also quite affordable. The more elaborate, unusual pieces command a higher price.

Harriet Spofford's Sampler, Massachusetts, 1814

Harriet's bold lettering in a dark color provides a good contrast to the lighter floral surround.

Birth records such as this are somewhat rare and highly collectible.

The dark thread has deteriorated and been absorbed into the ground fabric, adversely affecting the value.

The small dimensions of this piece enhance its value in the collectibles marketplace.

Size: 5¹/₂ x 6in/13.9 x 15.2cm
Value: $600–800

▶ *The fancy border that Harriet used to surround this silk on linen birth record adds to its charm and whimsical appeal.*

Sally Pomroy's Sampler, Massachusetts, 1819

The information Sally stitched is quite complete, including her name, age, date, and place—this increases value.

The sawtooth border gives a nice edge to the sampler and ensures that the piece was not cut from a larger sampler.

The central design is well-balanced and very well-stitched.

The flowers have faded from a brighter color to muted tones, which bears slightly on the value of the piece.

Size: 10 x 8in/
25.4 x 20.3cm
Value: $3,000–4,000

▶ *Sally showed considerable skill on her silk on linen sampler, especially for a seven-year-old child. She incorporated cross-stitch and long stitch in her nicely graphic pot of flowers, and she included this inscription:*
Sally Pomroy AE 7/
Salem January 19 1819.

▶ *This charming pictorial sampler was stitched by an unknown maker in the Boston area, c.1750–60. Worked in polychrome wool yarns on linen, it measures 9 × 7in/ 22.8 × 17.7cm and portrays a stag chased by a panting dog. Squirrels gather acorns in the oak tree. It was originally thought to be one of a kind, designed by the stitcher. But another needlework, showing the same scene, has recently surfaced. This suggests that both were made under the direction of one schoolmistress.*

Massachusetts
Essex County Samplers

In addition to the charming house and figure samplers of Essex County, MA, another style of sampler from the region—particularly from Boxford—was popular among needleworkers. Because the Essex County samplers resemble those from Middlesex County *(see pages 100–101)*, the two are often confused. Most notably, they both have deeply arcaded borders, usually on three sides. However, the delineating design on the Essex County pieces is more triangular than on the Middlesex pieces, and the spaces are decorated with floral motifs rather than geometric shapes.

Essex County needleworkers filled the centers of their samplers with standard alphabets and numbers. In the bottom panel, they often stitched pots of flowers and trees on hillocks, similar to those found on New Hampshire samplers *(see pages 114–119)*. In addition, they frequently filled in the borders of their designs with long New England laid stitch, creating a contrasting frame for the center alphabet section. These samplers are often large and usually worked on a dark ground fabric.

Their visual appeal and large size make Essex County samplers especially popular with collectors, even though there seem to be more of the Middlesex County type. The simplest explanation for the relative scarcity of Essex County samplers of this kind is that many Essex girls attended school in Boston. Designs in the Boston schools differed from those produced in the country schools; it is from the latter that these striking Essex designs emerged.

Sally Balch's Sampler, Massachusetts, *c.*1810

The sampler is unfinished, dark, and stained. It probably was not framed because it was not completed.

Note the coarse, dark, unbleached linen Sally used for her background fabric.

The choice to use muted colors against the dark ground makes the lettering difficult to read.

The lopsided pot of flowers and trees on hillocks add a charming note on the bottom panel.

Alone, Sally's sampler would not command a sizable price. Sold as a pair with her sister's sampler, however, it gains in value.

Size: 15³/₄ x 13in/40 x 33cm
Value: $2,000–3,000

Polly Balch's Sampler, Massachusetts, c.1810

Despite its unfinished state, Polly's work is much more enterprising than her sister's.

The deeply arcaded border is stitched overall in white, dramatically highlighting the floral design.

Because Polly worked her pot of flowers in such a colorful way, it stands out more than Sally's does.

Pairs of samplers worked by sisters tend to be rare, which increases the value of any that are found and sold together.

Size: 19 x 17in/48.2 x 43.2cm
Value: $4,500–5,500

▶ *Polly worked a larger sampler in silk on linen than did her sister. Oddly, like her sister, she did not complete her work.*

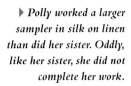

◀ *While living at Topsfield School in Boxford, Sally began a silk on linen sampler that was typical for the Essex County area. For some unknown reason, however, she did not complete her work.*

Genealogies of Sally and Polly Balch

The basic genealogical details of Sally and Polly Balch help give the collector a sense of place and time for these young needleworkers. They also provide value-enhancing provenance.

The girls were the daughters of David (1753–1812) and his second wife Sarah Peabody Balch (1769–1845). David's first wife died of consumption at age 22, in 1784, two years after their marriage and three months after the birth of their son David. The elder David married Sarah in 1786, and they had five children. David took his own life about sunset on July 22, 1812, and his widow died on March 2, 1845.

(Mary) Polly was born on March 7, 1792, and died on January 7, 1859. She married Henry Luscomb Jr. (1785–1837) of Salem—their "intentions" were filed on March 25, 1809, in Topsfield. They had 10 children, three of whom died young.

Sally was born on June 19, 1800, death date unknown. She married David Sanderson (b. 1796) of Salem in 1822. Their daughter, Lucy Ann, was born in Topsfield in about 1822.

Massachusetts Middlesex County Samplers

A vast number of samplers were produced in Middlesex County, MA, between 1750 and 1850. Measuring some 800 square miles, the region's population in 1820 was recorded as 61,476 persons. It included such important towns as Concord, Cambridge, Charlestown, Lexington, and Lowell, significant centers of learning and participation in the American Revolution.

Samplers of several types appeared in this area, each displaying particular characteristics. The most popular Middlesex County style features a deep, three-sided, arcaded border containing floral or geometric patterns within undulating lines. Leaves often protruded from the base line, while the bottom edge of the sampler remained without a border. The needleworker sometimes finished the bottom portion of the work with a floral grouping or a strawberry cartouche that enclosed the maker's name and the date of completion. Such pieces were not signed "Middlesex County," but research has identified that region as the residence of most of the makers.

Because so many of these samplers exist, it is improbable that they were made under the tutelage of just a few teachers. The border design may have been introduced to the region by one schoolmistress, copied by others, and then produced with numerous variations by students who themselves later became teachers in the area.

The Middlesex County samplers are striking and graphic, with deep borders that provide a pleasing contrast to the standard alphabet. Popular versions also include a house flanked by figures—these bring higher prices than those with geometric or floral patterns.

Nancy Simonds's Sampler, Massachusetts, 1800

The large four-sided flowers are presented in three different styles and color combinations.

The strawberry bands are also interpreted in several different styles, including double strawberries in the border.

The colors have faded to a mellow tone that detracts from the piece's value.

On the other hand, the sampler's value is enhanced by its overall visual appeal.

Size: 16 x 12³⁄₄ in/
40.6 x 32.3cm
Value: $3,000–4,000

▶ The side panels on Nancy's silk on linen sampler are quite unusual in design. They are also different from the top border, a treatment not often seen on samplers.

Chloe Trask's Sampler, Massachusetts, *c.*1800

The light-colored linen background is unusual and costlier than the standard unbleached linens more commonly used.

The double-heart motif used in the border evolved from a 17th-century band pattern.

The symmetry and matching colors throughout the body of the sampler and its border create wonderful balance.

Chloe stitched her name and year and later picked out the last two numbers of the date (women did not like to disclose their age even in that era).

Excellent condition makes this sampler highly prized.

Size: 17¼in/43.8cm sq
Value: $15,000–18,000

▶ This Middlesex sampler by Susanna Whittemore was part of the noted Joan Stephens collection, sold at Sotheby's in January 1997. One of a large group of house and figure samplers created in Middlesex County from 1790 to 1806, this silk on linen piece measures 22³/₈ × 15³/₈ / 56.8 × 39cm. It includes the common Middlesex County inscription: **The fairest flower will soon decay/ Its fragrance lose and splendid hue/ So youth and beauty wear away/ And vanish as the morning dew.**

▲ Chloe's bright and colorful silk on linen sampler has remained in spectacular condition. Her inscription is limited, but nonetheless helpful: **Time has wings and swiftly flies/ Youth and Beauty Fade away/ Virtue is the only Prize/ Whose Joys never will decay/ Chloe Trask's Work wrought in the year 18(??).**

Massachusetts House and Figure Samplers

Charming samplers displaying houses and female figures were made in great numbers in Massachusetts in the 19th century. Many can be identified regionally, while the origin of pieces made in more obscure country schools can be determined only if the maker can be reliably identified and researched. Occasionally, a single motif—such as the floral design in the center left of Lydia Hill's sampler *(below)*—may be the clue needed to pinpoint the sampler's origin.

While the house and figures are the dominant design elements on these samplers, needleworkers chose a variety of ways to position these motifs. Sometimes, the house is located at the bottom of the piece in the midst of a stitched expanse of grass. At other times, the house is placed above a four-sided border in the lower or central portion. The figures face forward or sideways and include both adults and children, hatted or bareheaded. Alphabets are usually located at the top of the work, sometimes accompanied by a verse or motto. Borders and decorative designs vary from region to region.

The house and figure piece, perhaps more than any other, reigns as the classic, traditional, and much sought after sampler—the design that springs to mind most readily when the subject of samplers arises. Despite the fact that such samplers are abundant, prices have increased greatly in the last few years.

Lydia Hill's Sampler, Massachusetts, 1790

A four-sided strawberry border makes a compact, finished edge to the piece.

The alphabet and dividing bands are neatly worked and varied in color.

The floral design in the left middle is typical of samplers from Middlesex County *(see Chloe Trask's sampler, page 101).*

While the childlike figures add to the value of this piece, the overall condition—slightly dark with faded threads—detracts.

Size: 10 x 8in/24.5 x 20.3cm
Value: $2,000–2,500

▶ *A Middlesex County girl, Lydia depicted three females, perhaps herself with her mother and sister, on this small, silk on linen sampler. Notice the pronounced disproportion between the figures and house.*

Sampler by "LB," Massachusetts, *c.*1795

The attractive corner blocks are worked in Queen stitch.

The color and condition are very good, always a plus for value.

The coarse linen ground fabric is typical of late 18th-century samplers from the Marblehead area, as are the colors, size, and design. Samplers from this area are highly prized.

The bottom panel contains an impressive three-story, center-hall house that is flanked by a side view of two young ladies.

Animals and bordering trees add visual interest.

Size: 16 x 12in/40.6 x 30.5cm
Value: $4,000–5,000

▶ *Probably from Marblehead, LB did not sign her silk on linen work. However, her inscription ensured that everyone knew her birth date: L B Born Dec/ 23 1782.*

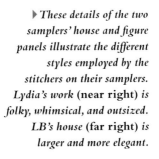

▶ *These details of the two samplers' house and figure panels illustrate the different styles employed by the stitchers on their samplers. Lydia's work (near right) is folky, whimsical, and outsized. LB's house (far right) is larger and more elegant.*

Massachusetts House Samplers

After floral designs, the most popular decorative motif found on 19th-century Massachusetts samplers is the house. Stitched in an array of architectural styles, colors, and shapes, the house signifies a familiar, secure place of comfort and happiness. Often, the house is a rendition of the sampler maker's home. Alternatively, it may represent the building that housed the maker's school. Whether in fact home or school, the motif is the main focus of the sampler's design and gives the overall piece an air of importance.

House samplers were pieces intended to be framed and hung as evidence of a schoolgirl's accomplishment. Because the house served as the major focal point, the needleworker would invest great care in the details of both the house and the landscape. Although most samplers of this period are dated, some are not. In such cases, the details of architectural style can often assist in determining the approximate date of the sampler's production.

Landscapes adjacent to the house also play an important role as design elements and reveal interesting personal information. A farm scene may depict the girl's family homestead; a village scene may indicate that the maker's father was a merchant. Obviously, such data can only be substantiated with further research, but the personal nature of the facts revealed makes the house sampler more interesting as Americana than artifacts without such personality.

Houses were stitched in great profusion on samplers of many regions, and there are literally thousands of these pieces in existence. Their pictorial quality makes them highly desirable, but their quantity keeps the market value at a relatively reasonable level.

Augusta March's Sampler, Massachusetts, 1822

Augusta used a sawtooth edge to divide the interior of the piece from its deep, luxurious, double-vined floral border.

The verse above the house is barely legible. If Augusta had used deeper colors, the otherwise good condition of this sampler would command a great deal more.

The center-hall, two-story house with paned windows and fenced garden also includes a porch sheltering two figures in the doorway.

The disproportionate birds, tree, and floral basket give the sampler a wonderfully folky feel.

Size: 16½in/41.9cm sq
Value: $5,000–6,000

Sally Wales Turner's Sampler, Massachusetts, *c.*1810

Sally's border is unusual and decorative. The rarity increases the sampler's value. The unusual oval shape suggests that, as in other samplers from the region, the outer edges were meant to be stitched in black.

The shape and style Sally intended to create on this piece emulate the reverse-painted black glass usually found on silk embroideries.

The large house with its adjacent orchard may well be a depiction of Sally's home.

Note the crooked but charming fence.

Size: 16 x 12in/40.6 x 30.5cm
Value: $6,000–8,000

▶ *Sally probably came from the Leominster area of Massachusetts. The fanciful border, which she stitched in a variety of asymmetrical designs, makes her silk on linen sampler truly unique.*

◀ *Augusta was born on February 4, 1805, the daughter of Tylor and Sally Marsh in Spencer, Worcester, MA. Her inscription reveals that she was 17 when she made this silk on linen sampler, not uncommonly old for girls in country schools.*

▶ *This detail from the sampler opposite shows the complex center-hall house with two chimneys. It features a hip roof, side columns, an elaborate porch, paned windows, and brown foundation stone. Note that the garden is neatly surrounded with a gated fence, creating an overall effect of serenity and friendliness.*

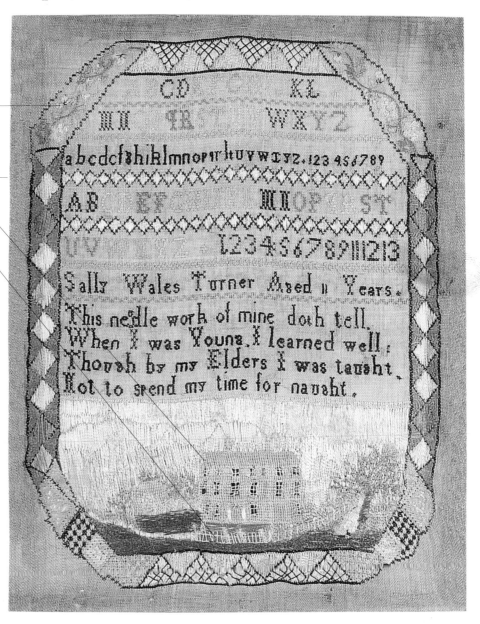

Massachusetts Floral Samplers

Floral motifs were popular design elements on samplers from all regions and all periods; even the earliest known needlework examples featured copies of botanical prints. In Massachusetts, sampler makers often included flowers both within the interior section of their pieces and to augment and decorate the border. Wide floral borders surrounding a squared-off interior consisting of alphabet, verse, and pictorial sections became popular in the 19th century. Although the strawberry border was by far the most common border in both the United States and Britain, floral designs can be found that include flowers and fruits of all varieties. In New England, grapes appeared frequently on borders and in panels, particularly in Middlesex County.

Flower arrangements on samplers probably became popular, in part, because they offered the stitcher relief from the usual cross-stitch used for letters and numbers. By incorporating a floral design, the maker could demonstrate her skill in a wide variety of stitches, while making the sampler a more interesting finished piece. Grapes and flowers, with leaves and tendrils, offered more challenge than the counted cross-stitch—a much-repeated process of stitching two threads over and two threads down.

Floral samplers are not uncommon. In assessing the value of one of these pretty pieces, the collector should look for variety of design, a strong pictorial panel, and good color throughout. As always, visual appeal and condition are of prime importance.

Sarah Crosby's Sampler, Massachusetts, 1812

The border displays the deeply arcaded style that was typical of Middlesex County.

More unusual are the wildflowers interspersed throughout the border.

The lettering is somewhat light in comparison to the floral motifs and may detract from the value of the piece.

Sarah's center panel is eye-catching and colorful, worked with silk thread in a long-stitch that gives a shimmery look to the flowers.

The floral borders and panel add to the value of what is essentially an alphabet marking sampler.

Sizes: 16³/₈ x 15in/
41.6 x38.1cm
Value: $3,000–4,000

Dolly Stone's Sampler, Massachusetts, 1819

Dolly's sampler, made in Middlesex County, includes grapes worked as a three-sided border design.

The generous size of the border sets off the interior.

Some of the lettering has little contrast to the background linen, making the inscription slightly difficult to read.

The overall condition is good, and the composition more interesting than the piece opposite.

The panel with center-hall house and landscape adds a simple but artistic quality to the overall design.

Size: unknown
Value: $4,000–5,000

▸ *Dolly Hariot Stone was born June 23, 1805, in Wayland, Middlesex County, MA, daughter of Israel Stone. She inscribed her sampler with this verse:* **When death dissolves the dearest ties/ And Love stands mourning o'er the bier/ What luster shines in Beauty's eyes/ Formed by Lilys sparkling Tear.**

▸ *This detail of the bouquet on the sampler opposite shows the lustrous quality of Sarah's crimped silk long stitch.*

◂ *Research has revealed that Sarah was born on September 15, 1798, the daughter of Ephraim and Sarah French Crosby in Billerica, Middlesex County, MA. The inscription on her silk on linen sampler states simply that she made it: . . . in the/ fourteenth year of her age 1812.*

Massachusetts Family Record Samplers

In the late 18th century, a new type of sampler appeared. Referred to as family records, family registers, or genealogies, these samplers were made at schools in the same way as other types of samplers. Unlike the typical samplers of earlier years that focused on such design elements as alphabet, verse, and pictures, these samplers were created primarily to record the births, deaths, and marriages of the immediate family. Some were quite simplistic in design, as is illustrated by the Fillebrown piece below. Others were heavily embellished with designs and verse, as in the Daniels record at right. Often the death and marriage portion were filled in at a later date by either the maker or another stitcher.

Because of the information contained on these samplers, needleworkers often compartmentalized their design, allowing a column each for names, births, and deaths. In some cases, both birth dates and marriage dates of siblings were included. The vast amount of data is a great help in researching family histories. However, if the maker failed to sign her work and if her family included more than one female child, then the maker's identity can, and often does, remain a mystery.

Until recently, collectors did not gravitate toward these family records. With new research, though, and with greater emphasis on genealogy in general, collectors have come to pay more attention to these stitched histories. The samplers were particularly popular in northern New England and therefore are not scarce today. The more complete records leave little background linen unstitched, making them quite appealing.

Family Register of Samuel and Dorcas Fillebrown, Massachusetts, c.1820

The floral border, surrounding sawtooth border, and arched floral decorations are expertly stitched and shaded.

Dorcas was born in 1784 and son Samuel in 1802, indicating that Dorcas married at quite a young age.

Which of the four daughters made this family register is unknown; more than likely, it was not Mary, whose birth is stitched in a different hand.

This register does not have the visual appeal of the one opposite. The blank sections and lack of contrasting, bright colors detract from the overall design.

Size: 16in/40.6cm sq
Value: $2,000–3,000

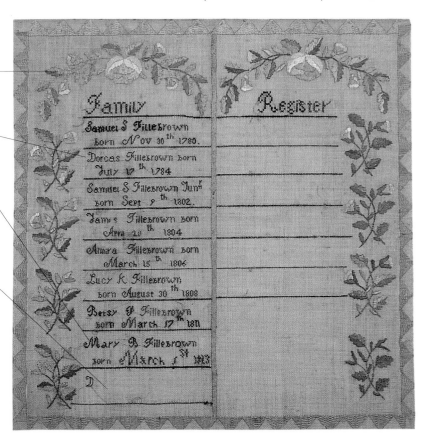

Susan E. Daniels's Family Record, Massachusetts, 1835

This sampler is very well-designed with strong visual impact.

The dark leaves of the flowers alternating with grape clusters make an unusual design.

The toning on the ground linen and the overall darkening reduce the value of this piece.

Susan combined a family record with a memorial that was completed at a later date.

The monument and weeping willows are memorial motifs in reference to Susan's father and brother, both of whom died after she stitched the birth dates in 1835.

Size: 22⅝ x 17⅛in/
57.4 x 43.5cm
Value: $7,000–9,000

▶ *Susan worked this silk on linen piece at the age of 12. The oldest of seven children, she recorded not only the births of her siblings but those of her parents as well. By leaving out their marriage date, she drew as little attention as possible to her arrival three months later.*

◀ *The silk on linen family register of Samuel and Dorcas Fillebrown of Cambridge, MA, records that they had six children. Note, however, that a sole letter "D" appears in the bottom space, raising the question as to whether more children were born after the making of this register.*

Notes on Family Records

Gloria Seaman Allen's 1989 exhibition catalog, entitled *Family Record, Genealogical Watercolors and Needlework*, presents fascinating insights into the structure of the American family from the 18th into the 19th century. Using 131 family records, both watercolor and stitched, Allen demonstrates a marked increase in family stability in the 19th century, with couples marrying later, having fewer children, and living longer. In this and other ways, she illustrates the historical value of these homespun records.

Massachusetts Family Records—Interpreting History

Family record samplers reached their peak in popularity between 1820 and 1830, especially in Massachusetts, where they were produced in large numbers. Despite the quantity, it's possible to attribute a specific place or teacher to many of these samplers because of regional differences in design and because small groups of the pieces show sufficient similarities and common characteristics. Several pieces, for example, have surfaced that display a rosebud border outlined by a half-circle vine, as seen in the sampler from Wellfleet, MA, at right.

The social history of the period in which these samplers were produced is perhaps the most interesting aspect of the family record. Unlike samplers from the 17th and 18th centuries, which were sometimes dotted with the initials of parents, grandparents, and members of the extended family, the 19th-century family register focused on immediate family, parents, and offspring. By carefully reading the inscriptions and dates, it is often possible not only to locate the sampler's origin, but also to interpret the history of the family. A mother's death shortly after childbirth probably relates to that event; multiple deaths of children in close proximity often indicate a regional epidemic or contagious disease in the home. The more information recorded on a sampler, the greater its value will be to a collection, especially if the piece is well-designed and in good condition.

Abigail Rich's Family Register, Massachusetts, 1829

Neatly compartmentalized, the information recorded on this piece is easy to read and decipher.

As Abigail included no particular name, initials, or date in the memorial, it is unclear if she worked this in remembrance of a specific person.

The urn-and-willow memorial design was traditional and found on many examples from this time and place.

Condition problems—in this case, faded thread and slight staining—detract from the price.

Size: 18³/₄ x 16¹/₂ in/
47.6 x 41.9cm
Value: $4,000–5,000

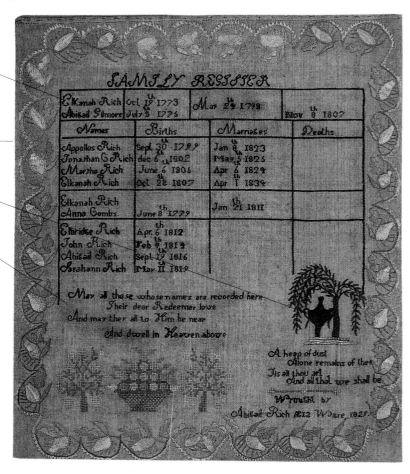

Maria G. Atwood's Family Record, Massachusetts, 1829

Maria stitched a well-developed, nicely composed family record.

The large floral border with corner flowers is not typically found on family registers.

The columns, found on other samplers from this area of Cape Cod, enclose the name and birth dates of the children, while the parents' names, birth and marriage dates appear above.

The lettering on the memorial to Maria's sister is artistically and gracefully overstitched.

Colorful and in excellent condition, this is an exceptional family register.

Size: 16 x 24in/
40.6 x 61cm
Value: $10,000–12,000

▶ *Maria's ancestry dates back to Frances Cooke, who came to North America on the Mayflower and was one of the signers of the Mayflower Compact. Maria stitched her silk on linen piece when she was 11 years old and living in Wellfleet, MA.*

◀ *Abigail Rich was 12 years old when she stitched this silk on linen sampler. She was the daughter of Elkhanah and Anna Coombs Rich. Elkhanah's first wife, Abigail Gilmore Rich, died in 1807 at the age of 32, eleven days after the birth of her fourth child.*

◀ *This silk on linen piece (16 × 14in/40.6 × 35.5cm) by Clarissa Harrington is exceptional in color, detail, and design. There are numerous apple-tree registers known to have originated in Middlesex County, MA. Typical of a design taught by an unknown schoolmistress, the yellow apples represent the births of Clarissa's sisters, and the white apple the birth of her brother.*

Massachusetts
Newburyport Samplers

The town of Newburyport, located north of Boston and noted for its commerce and shipbuilding, was also the home of several schools for young ladies and produced many samplers and embroideries. Being a coastal town near a major city, many of its designs bear a resemblance to patterns found in Boston area samplers. Although band samplers were not the norm in the early 19th century, many band-type examples were worked in Newbury and Newburyport (the two towns were united until 1764) during this period.

One of the most popular bands worked in Newburyport was the trefoil motif. A carryover from English patterns, this band is found in other areas but seemed to enjoy special prominence here. Diamond bands, carnations, and hearts, along with geometric motifs, appeared regularly. The two examples shown on these pages provide an excellent overview of the various stitching and color choices that give these bands their unique visual appeal. Floral designs were used extensively, often wildly spilling from a blue vase or hillock.

The colorful presentation and variety of these samplers make them very appealing pieces to collect. Earlier pieces from the 18th-century school of Ann Waters are especially dynamic and include large parrots. They are highly sought after by advanced collectors and can be quite expensive. But many less expensive examples exist that have been beautifully stitched and colorfully rendered. Such pieces are a good investment and addition to a collection.

Hannah Pike's Sampler, Massachusetts, 1823

An attractive sampler, this is an excellent choice for a beginning collector.

The overall condition is good, although there is slight fading to the silk floss.

The carnation, heart, and flower bands are found extensively on other samplers from this area.

Both Hannah and Abigail *(opposite)* stitched the most common verse found on samplers.

Trefoil bands were popular designs used for both borders and divisions on Newburyport samplers, making this an identifiable example.

Size: 16½ x 10½in/
41.9 x 26.6cm
Value: $1,800–2,500

▶ *Hannah worked her pretty, borderless sampler in silk on linen, using a variety of border designs as band patterns.*

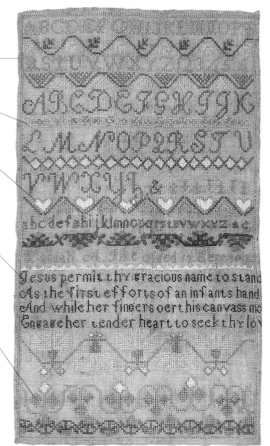

Abigail Cook's Sampler, Massachusetts, 1827

Four alphabets are worked in different stitches and styles and are separated by decorative bands.

The trefoil band is common to the area; Abigail stitched it with a pattern within each leaf.

The block letters are placed in an unusual arrangement.

The rose-and-tree panel is nicely balanced, using different trees that Hannah has placed on hillocks.

This is an attractive sampler that incorporates a variety of designs, enhancing its value.

Size: 17 x 16½in/
43.1 x 41.9cm
Value: $5,000–6,000

▶ *Abigail stitched the same popular verse on her silk on linen sampler as Hannah did (opposite), but her spelling is notably lacking in accuracy.*

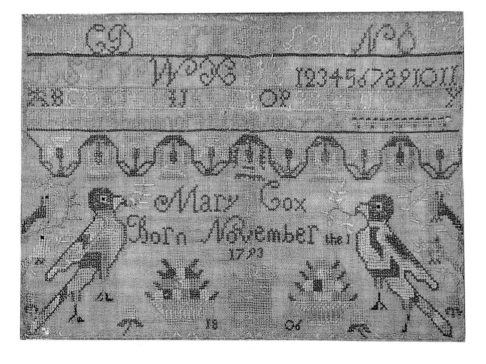

▶ *This silk on linen sampler (10 × 14in/25.4 × 35.5cm) by Mary Cox features two large facing parrots. This motif was found on many samplers worked under the tutelage of Ann Waters, a teacher in Newburyport in the late 18th and early 19th centuries. The birds add strong visual appeal to a sampler that would otherwise be an ordinary exercise.*

New Hampshire Canterbury Flower Basket Samplers

Public school students in the Canterbury, NH, area produced a huge number of samplers from the 1780s through the 1830s. Known as "Canterbury" pieces, the designs evolved from basic patterns created by schoolmistresses in the early post-Colonial period. These samplers are available in many design variations, making them a particular pleasure to collectors.

An important characteristic of this group of samplers is the large basket placed in the center of the bottom panel. The one-handled basket is flanked with leaves and holds an array of long-stemmed flowers. Typically, a pair of leaves rides above the center flower in the basket. The basket itself is situated on a band of hillocks strewn with flowers and flanked by two pine trees. On the more elaborate

pieces, pots of flowers and vines trail up the sides of the basket. Needleworkers often portrayed birds holding the paired leaves or decorating the top or bottom borders. Among the Canterbury samplers' most outstanding features is the black outlining of the border elements. A double-vined strawberry band often appears, either running through the center of the sampler to separate alphabets, or, on simpler pieces, as a four-sided border.

Research shows that many of the young sampler makers eventually became teachers who in turn handed down the traditional patterns they stitched on their samplers as students. Canterbury samplers are highly prized by collectors and can command high prices if well-composed and in excellent condition.

Betsy Stevens's Sampler, New Hampshire, 1796

The white sawtooth border frames this sampler nicely.

The strawberry band is worked in unusually bright colors.

Although charming and from the same school as Abigail's sampler *(opposite)*, Betsy's piece is not as grand or valuable.

The blank area was most likely intended to contain a matching basket of flowers as seen on the left.

Size: 14 x 16in/35.5 x 40.6cm
Value: $8,000–12,000

▶ *Although Betsy's silk on linen sampler is an earlier Canterbury piece, it exhibits many of the motifs found in later samplers. Born on December 8, 1783, to Simon and Elizabeth Boynton Stevens, Betsy went on to marry Samuel Sargent, the son of a Canterbury teacher.*

Abigail French's Sampler, New Hampshire, 1822

Abigail worked a fully-developed border around the central alphabets on her silk on linen sampler.

Outside borders decorated with leafy flowers in stylized pots further enhance the overall design.

The large strawberry band separating the two alphabets adds interest to the text panel.

Note the main motif, consisting of a basket with paired leaves flanked by birds and stick pines, all atop rolling hillocks outlined in black.

The overall appearance is exuberant and rich.

Size: 16³/8 x 17¹/8 in/
41.6 x 43.5cm
Value: $40,000–$50,000

▶ *Like Abigail, most public school stitchers tended to be older than private school sampler makers. Her inscription reads:* Abigail French's Sampler wrought in the Seventeenth/ year of her Age A x d 1822.

▶ *This detail of Abigail's basket panel shows her dramatic handling of shaded tones and black outlining.*

New Hampshire Floral Samplers

Meandering floral borders are characteristic of New Hampshire samplers. Found in a variety of styles, they employ various stitches that tested the skill of young sampler makers. They also serve to neatly frame the interior of the needlework. These floral designs were first drawn onto the ground fabric, then embroidered, rather than worked in the traditional sampler cross-stitch.

Regional differences can often be seen in the design elements and background fabric of these samplers. Such details allow the knowledgeable collector to trace a sampler's origin when inscriptions are incomplete.

Floral borders can be three-sided or total surrounds, either symmetrical or asymmetrical. Most of the borders have an undulating vine sprouting a variety of flowers, leaves, and buds. This treatment was typical in the first half of the 19th century, with variations found on samplers from throughout the United States. Over time, collectors learn through observation and comparison to recognize not only the specific regional differences, but also the general time frame in which these samplers were produced.

Fanciful, often delicate, and quite pretty, floral bordered samplers make very attractive additions to any collection. Their sizes and content vary significantly, allowing the collector to accumulate a great many of them without duplicating any design.

Rebeckah Bacon's Sampler, New Hampshire, 1828

Rebeckah left her needle and thread in the upper left-hand corner of her unfinished record.

The family record is neatly compartmentalized, with a filled-in sawtooth border and further cartouches separating parents from children.

Rebeckah stitched the most popular verse found on samplers, although she omitted the word "tender" (before "heart") in the last line.

The overall condition is good, with little staining and only slight fading.

Size: approx. 16 x 17in/ 40.6 x 43.2cm
Value: $6,000–8,000

▶ *Created in Jaffrey, NH, when Rebeckah was 11 years old, her silk on linen family register is nicely executed with a beautiful flowery vine border, surrounding the recorded genealogy.*

Eliza Wallis's Sampler, New Hampshire, 1817

Beautifully executed in shades of greens and browns on a light linen ground, the composition of this piece is startlingly fresh.

The meandering floral border is well designed.

Eliza stitched an inner sawtooth border to set the content apart.

Design elements fill empty spaces within the cartouche and verse.

Visual charm and excellent condition make this an exceptional example.

Size: 15¹/₈ x 19¹/₈ in/
38.4 x 48.5cm
Value: $15,000–17,000

▶ *Eliza, daughter of Arthur and Elisabeth McIntosh Wallace, completed her silk on linen gauze sampler in Brookline, NH. Variant spellings of names—"Wallis" and "Wallace"—were not uncommon and were often used interchangeably.*

◀ *The upper detail at left shows how the dark green leaves from Eliza's central design (above) create a sharp contrast to the sprigs of flowers in crimped silk thread. Against a field of white linen, the effect is quite dramatic. Compare this to the lower close-up, which shows the relatively quieter appearance of the bottom border from Rebeckah's work (opposite). Such touches can affect the value of a piece on the collectibles market.*

New Hampshire Green Linsey-Woolsey Samplers

The green linsey-woolsey samplers of northeastern New England are strikingly attractive. They were worked in silk on a green ground fabric consisting of a linen warp and a wool weft. Most examples come from northeast Massachusetts, New Hampshire, and coastal Maine. This fabric was occasionally used in other areas.

Linsey-woolsey fabric was often produced at home, although it was sometimes purchased from a professional weaver. Most often, homemakers used the fabric for bedcovers referred to as "linsey-woolsies." For these linens, the women quilted together two thicknesses of fabric, the top layer a linsey-woolsey weave and the bottom layer wool, with wool batting sandwiched between. These linsey-woolsies were dyed in an array of colors, most commonly green. Sampler makers used these same materials for their ground fabrics, sometimes choosing a scrap of the wide bedcover fabric; in this case, the sampler would be hemmed on four sides. At other times, the fabric must have been intended for some other household use, as the loom width was narrower from the start.

Green samplers provide some of the rarest and most highly sought New Hampshire samplers. Linsey-woolsey frequently suffers some background loss due to insect damage and the nature of the fabric. If minor, this does not affect the value unduly; however, large or abundant holes will bring the value down.

Ann Trash's Sampler, New Hampshire, c. 1800

Ann's sampler features a carnation border that enhances the piece nicely.

The green background creates much-needed contrast in this piece.

Ann's verse is not as carefully stitched as the alphabet and border, but lends a schoolgirl charm to the overall composition.

Pretty and decorative, the sampler is not a high-end example, but is certainly collectible.

Size: 22 x 10³/₄ in/
55.9 x 27.3cm
Value: $4,500–5,500

▶ *Ann chose a monochromatic color scheme for her silk on linsey-woolsey sampler, which would be quite boring and unreadable had she worked it on the typical linen ground.*

Eunice Ladd's Sampler, New Hampshire, *c.*1810

Eunice's dark green background gives great depth to her composition, worked chiefly in light and blue colors.

Eyelet stitching used for the blue alphabet shows skill with the needle and offers a nice variation.

The basket and trees are typical New Hampshire motifs often found on samplers from the Canterbury area.

Note that Eunice left the fruit basket on the left unfinished.

The deeper background and stronger contrast in color and design make this sampler a more valuable piece than Ann's *(opposite)*.

Size: 15¹/₂ x 17³/₄in/
39.3 x 45cm
Value: $6,000–8,000

▲ Eunice stitched a very precise and dramatic sampler in silk on green linsey-woolsey. Research suggests that she probably produced this in Portsmouth, NH.

◄ ▲ *Details from the two samplers on these pages illustrate one aspect that can affect relative value. Note how Eunice has worked her flowers* (above) *in multilayers, giving them a depth and dramatic appeal lacking in Ann's flat, two-dimensional flowers (left).*

New Hampshire House and Animal Samplers

Pictorial samplers are evocative and very charming, factors that make them highly collectible in today's market. Unlike earlier band samplers, the pictorial samplers included depictions of houses, buildings, people, and animals. Abundant in New Hampshire and worked by girls of all ages, means, and regions, these pieces are often the most elementary and interesting of all the samplers collected today.

Many of the pictorial samplers were worked at country schools. At such schools, the teachers came and went with some frequency and more likely than not lacked great skill in the needle arts. As a result, the samplers stitched under their direction have a primitive and folky feel that is much admired and appreciated by collectors.

Borders on such samplers are often limited to three sides only, so that a landscape scene could be fully developed at the bottom without the distraction of the underlying border. Often, these rural samplers include peculiar arrangements of design elements, while alphabets and numbers are sometimes configured in unusual ways. Although alphabets were usually stitched in the traditional manner, other elements would reflect the individual style of the sampler maker.

New Hampshire samplers with houses and figures comprise a large and engaging group. Readily available, they range in price from a few thousand dollars to tens of thousands, depending on the artistic presentation, color, and condition of the work.

Lucy Duncklee's Sampler, New Hampshire, c.1829

Lucy's numbers beginning in the second line and ending in the last line include a backward 10.

The border is attractively stitched and frames the interior with big round polka-dot flowers.

Lucy's verse is somewhat elementary in execution, suggesting that she may have been quite young when she did this work.

The animals are wonderfully disproportionate, adding charm and value to the sampler.

Size: 16¼ x 17¾in/
41.2 x 45cm
Value: $4,000–5,000

Ann Fisher's Sampler, probably New Hampshire, *c.*1807

Note how the border is interspersed with alphabets and numbers in a most unusual arrangement.

Ann's inclusion of her teacher's name is important in terms of the sampler's value on the market.

The house and outbuilding panel, with dovecote, is quite typical of New Hampshire samplers.

Colorful and in good condition, this sampler also has good design qualities.

Size: 15 x 16¼in/
38.1 x 41.2cm
Value: $5,000–6,000

▶ *Although Ann was born in Maine near the mouth of the Kennebec River, she may have made this silk on linen sampler in New Hampshire, or under the tutelage of a teacher who had studied there.*

▶ *Lucy stitched the three folky animals, seen in the detail at right, in sizes that are disproportionate to the house on her sampler (opposite). The spotted animal sets off the panel and creates a visual liveliness important to the piece.*

◀ *Lucy was born February 27, 1819, one of five children born to Hezekiah and Anna Bachelder Duncklee. She married Stephen Carleton of Nashua and died on February 2, 1888. She worked this silk on linen piece in Lyndeborough, NH, probably at about age 10.*

Rhode Island House and Figure Samplers

Rhode Island samplers worked in Providence and Newport in the last quarter of the 18th century and early 19th century are some of the most charming and sought-after needleworks available today. Peppered with figures, stately buildings, and houses, they command extraordinary prices when found in good condition. There are, however, many less-developed examples that collectors can acquire for less astronomical prices.

Like all samplers, Rhode Island pieces were stitched to learn marking and to make an attractive presentation piece. The style of these samplers sets them apart from other samplers made elsewhere in New England. Usually worked in bands, the alphabets, names, and dates were interspersed with colorful panels of large and small figures, often flanking houses. Proportions were not considered important, and consequently gigantic flowers can tower over little people, or large people can overpower a two-story house. Verses are often simple, incorporating a variety of stitches, especially on those pieces worked at Mary Balch's school in Providence.

Because of their exquisite charm, these Rhode Island samplers are highly prized and collected. Some of the samplers are quite small but still visually appealing, thanks to the figures and overall pictorial quality.

Ruth Hazard's Sampler, Rhode Island, 1791

This small sampler is rather simple for a girl of 14 years.

The charm of the central panel enhances the value of this piece.

The large two-story, center-hall house with six windows on the second floor is an imposing structure that adds considerable visual interest to the piece.

Ruth added wonderful details to her colonial costumes, complete with buttons and lace trim.

Size: 12 x 8½in/
30.4 x 21.6cm
Value: $4,000–5,000

▶ *Ruth's charming silk on linen sampler depicts disproportionately large people. Note that she also misspelled some words in the verse.*

Catharine Sabin's Sampler, Rhode Island, *c.*1800

Catharine did not finish her strawberry band, worked in Queen stitch; the background should have been completely filled in.

The ground fabric is stained and has browned from acidity in the backboard, which detracts from the sampler's value.

The bottom panel is wonderfully pictorial, with small people and disproportionately large flowers.

Despite condition issues, Balch School pieces such as this are highly desirable.

Size: 13⅝ x 12/
34.6 x 30.4cm
Value: $5,500–6,500

▶ *The verse, strawberry band, and pictorial band on Catharine's silk on linen sampler are all value-adding elements typical of samplers worked under the instruction of Mary Balch.*

▼ *The figures stitched on both samplers are important design elements. Ruth's elaborate costumes (below left) give her couple distinction. Catharine's facing couple are clad elegantly and given walking sticks.*

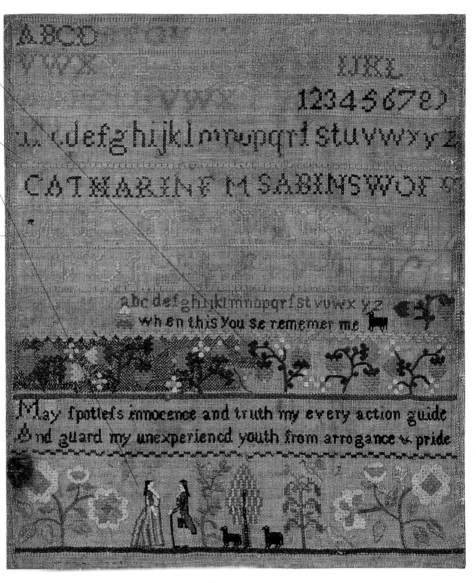

Rhode Island Providence Samplers

Samplers worked at the Mary Balch School in Providence, RI, make up a very important group of samplers. Known for their distinctive figures and buildings, they are pictorial in design and skillfully worked. The sampler makers often featured stately houses or important buildings. These included such imposing edifices as Rhode Island College (now called the University Hall of Brown University), the First Baptist Meetinghouse, the First Congregational Church, and the Providence State House.

Mary Balch began teaching in 1782 to help her mother meet expenses after her father died, and her school

lasted for 45 years. Because of the school's long life, its students over the years produced a large body of work, encompassing simple marking samplers, exquisite pictorial samplers, and silk embroideries of many types.

The elaborate pieces from Mary's school—with their overall stitching and graphic elements—command strong prices in the retail market. Simpler pieces, however, can often be found and purchased at a fraction of the cost. Because of the important research published by Betty Ring in *Let Virtue Be a Guide to Thee,* much is known about Mary Balch, her family, and her school, making these samplers some of the most highly sought after.

Leafea Ide's Sampler, Rhode Island, 1796

This piece is dark, due to the unbleached linen on which it was worked and the exposure to acidic backing material, all of which affects its value.

Leafea filled in empty spaces in the inscription and tree lines with odd little animals and figures.

The figures that appear in the windows add interest and perhaps represent girls boarding at the home of Mary Balch.

The bottom panel of house and courting couples is quite typical of the work stitched at Mary Balch's school.

Staining and fading affect the assessed value of this piece. However, the fact that it is an 18th-century Providence sampler enhances the value.

Size: 16¼in/41.2cm sq
Value: $4,000–5,000

Betsy Davis's Sampler, Rhode Island, 1794

Betsy worked an attractive sampler with a wide strawberry band in the center. Often found on Balch School pieces, this band sometimes had a solidly stitched background.

Betsy included her name, age, date, and location—important information for both additional research and value.

Her verse was somewhat ambitious for the space available; as a consequence, words are squeezed in and placed above or below the verse line.

Minor thread loss and fading detract slightly from the value of this sampler.

Size: 11 x 8in/
27.9 x 20.3cm
Value: $5,000–6,000

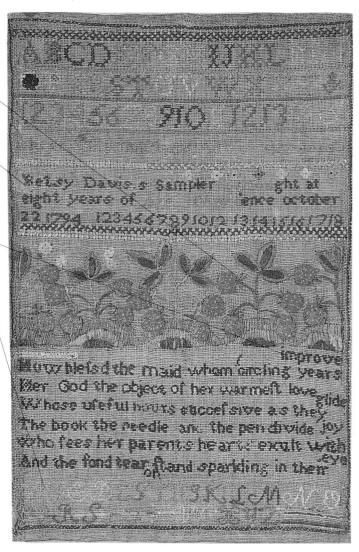

▶ It is known that Betsy stitched this silk on linen piece at Mary Balch's school. She also worked an elaborate silk embroidery during her years there.

◀ Leafea was the daughter of Jacob and Lydia Kent Ide of Attleborough, MA (located twelve miles from Providence), but she stitched her silk on linen work in Providence, RI. She married Eli Bourn on November 30, 1809, in Attleborough.

◀ Mary Hall created this important silk on linen Balch School piece (16 × 12in/40.6 × 30.4cm) in c.1806. It contains all the bells and whistles—large center house with fence, peopled bands with trees and animals, tall, striped, and arched columns, elaborately worked floral borders of Queen stitch, classic inscription below paired angels and heart, and characteristic strawberry band. All in all, it is a wonderful presentation.

Rhode Island Building Samplers

Rhode Island was the home of numerous schools providing instruction in needlework, and samplers that depicted buildings were popular in many of them. In particular, the Mary Balch School in Providence produced numerous samplers that featured magnificent buildings. Other schools' samplers included houses, churches, and other edifices, but generally without the dramatic presentation of the Balch School pieces.

Buildings appeared on samplers in Europe and America from the early 18th to the mid 19th century. Architectural features stitched on needlework provide the piece with a focal point that adds considerable interest not only for the viewer, but for the stitcher as well. These stitched buildings also include a hidden benefit. Regional differences in architectural design often help the collector identify the origins of the pieces on which they appear.

Rhode Island samplers—especially those from Providence—tend to include public buildings more than those from other regions. The inclusion of a building can add value to an ordinary sampler, as we see in the piece below. The more interesting and detailed the structure, the more desirable the piece becomes. Additional elements such as figures, verse, and borders, further enhance collectors' choice.

Anonymous State Building Sampler, Rhode Island, c. 1800

The crudeness of this sampler suggests that the maker was either very young or relatively unskilled.

The poor condition of the lettering is detrimental to the piece's value.

The building on this sampler seems to pop out from the background to dominate the small sampler.

The building is solidly stitched and includes considerable detail for such a simple piece.

The exceptional building makes this a rare and collectible needlework.

Size: approx. 15 x 9in/
38.1 x 22.8cm
Value: $1,500–2,500

▶ *This silk on linen sampler almost certainly came from Rhode Island. Although the lettering is unreadable, the striking building is typical of work from that state.*

Ruth Smith's Sampler, Rhode Island, 1799

Note that she included her parents' initials in the top corners of the piece.

The color is strong and contrasting, and the design is pleasing.

Ruth stitched an unusual border with clumps of unconnected flowers.

The overall condition is quite good, and such an 18th-century Rhode Island sampler is highly sought-after, adding significant value.

It appears that Ruth did not quite finish her sampler. The windows lack panes, and she may have planned to cover the ground fabric in the bottom portion as she did the top.

Size: 14½ x 12in/
35.5 x 30.4cm
Value: $6,000–8,000

◀ This detail of the top of the building on the sampler opposite shows the exceptional amount of attention the maker invested in her work. This is all the more notable, given the relative simplicity of the piece.

▲ Ruth, daughter of Samuel and Phebe Pearce Smith of Bristol, inscribed her silk on linen with a moralistic verse: **Let Spotless Innocence and Truth/ My Every Action Guide/ And Guide My Unexperienced Youth/ From Vanity And Pride.**

Vermont
Marking Samplers

Vermont produced fewer samplers than any other New England state. Sparsely settled—especially after the Revolutionary War, when many Vermonters moved to Canada out of loyalty to the British Crown—Vermont sent many of its more well-to-do girls to the fashionable young ladies' schools in Massachusetts, Connecticut, and Rhode Island to continue their studies and pursue the genteel arts. As a result, most of the Vermont samplers on the market today are simpler marking samplers worked at country schools by younger girls before they left for the more sophisticated schools elsewhere. Or they are pieces created by poorer girls who stayed at home in Vermont.

Regional differences are not as noticeable among Vermont samplers. The simplicity of these pieces rarely allows for unique expression or identifiable styles. Few 18th-century pieces exist, and those from the 19th century tend to be modest. On the other hand, these samplers often contain an abundance of pertinent information, including origin. It is not uncommon for Vermont samplers to include the name of the maker, her age, the date that she made her piece, the place where she made it, and the name of her teacher.

The marking samplers of Vermont contain a minimum of decorative motifs, usually limited to simple alphabets, numbers, and perhaps an elementary rendition of a house, flowers, or trees. They are often borderless and worked in a band format. Stitched lines underline each row of alphabet on many of the samplers. The background materials are of various types of homespun that were brought from home—often small pieces left over from a household textile project or recycled from a much-used object.

The sampler by Naomi Parker (opposite) demonstrates a very complete Vermont marking sampler. The alphabets are worked in various styles and underlined with rows of different stitches. Naomi inscribed her whole name, followed by a verse, another inscription, the year the sampler was completed, the name of her instructress, and the town where she made the piece. In 1830, Clarendon, VT, had a population of just over 1,500 people and 13,000 sheep. In this rural setting, Naomi stitched her work.

Due to their scarcity, Vermont pieces are much in demand among collectors. Samplers with pictorial decoration and information command higher prices, and as always, condition remains an important factor in determining the work's value.

Olive Reynolds's Sampler, Vermont, 1827

The horizontal shape seen here is common among Vermont samplers of this period.

Although she made a simple sampler, Olive used her colors creatively and altered the lettering in her alphabets.

Flanked by trees and featuring open side windows and an eyebrow window over the door, the house is an attractive touch.

Nicely stitched and in good condition, this is a very collectible needlework.

Size: 7³/₄ x 17³/₄ in/
19.6 x 45cm
Value: $1,800–2,500

Naomi Parker's Sampler, Vermont, 1824

Naomi included six alphabets on her sampler, including one worked in eyelet stitch.

Perhaps to highlight her hard work, Naomi boldly stitched "INDUSTRY" above the last alphabet.

Note her stitched designation "ensampler"—as opposed to "sampler"—a carryover from an earlier era.

Always important, but seldom noted by young sampler makers, is the instructress's name and place of origin.

Size: approx. 15 x 22in/ 38.1 x 55.8cm
Value: $3,000–4,000

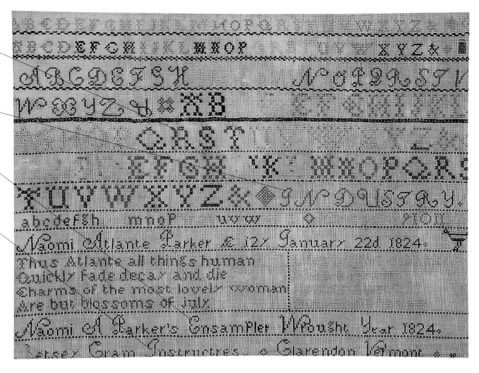

▶ *Naomi stitched an ambitious marking sampler in silk on linen, complete with alphabets, verse, and the details of her name, date, birth, and instructress:* Naomi Atlante Parker AE 12y January 22d 1824/ Thus Atlante all things human/ Quickly fade decay and die/ Charms of the most lovely woman/ Are but blossoms of july./ Naomi A. Parker's Ensampler Wrought Year 1824/ Betsey Cram Instructress, Clarendon Vermont.

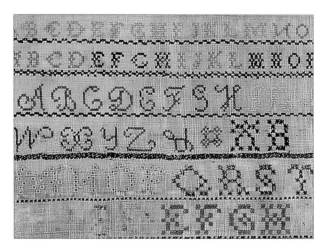

◀ *Notice in this detail the variety of letter treatments Naomi included on her sampler (above). Presumably, she would have chosen different types of lettering depending on the article she was marking—hence the need to practice.*

◀ *Olive Parker Reynolds stitched the inscription on her silk on linen sampler in a slightly confusing manner, but did manage to record pertinent information:* 1827/ Olive Parker years/ Reynolds Age 11/ Londonderry.

◀ *This detail shows the small center-hall Cape house, typical of rural Vermont, that Olive stitched on her sampler (opposite). The various colored windows may indicate that she ran out of a color; or it may have been a deliberate design choice.*

▶ Phoebe Ann House's Sampler, Washington Boro, PA, 1826. Phoebe's sampler represents one of the most graphic pieces from this region. Worked in silk, wool, and spangles on linen, it is filled with luxuriant flowering borders and features a central scene of house and garden. This sampler invites one to sit with Phoebe in the garden. The condition is superb and the quote uplifting. 21³/₈ × 24¹/₈ in / 54.2 × 61.2cm.

North American Samplers:
Mid-Atlantic & Southern

New Jersey House Samplers

As documented in *American Samplers,* the well-known reference book by Bolton and Coe, published in 1921, Massachusetts produced more samplers than any other state. The next most prolific state was New Jersey. As in other states, New Jersey sampler makers favored the house motif in its many variations. They would stitch the house in the bottom panel on a stepped hillock, with plants of one kind or another and sheep and other animals in the foreground.

Like other 19th-century samplers, New Jersey samplers often included alphabets worked in Queen stitch, flowers, geometric patterns, and borders. New Jersey samplers also bear a close resemblance to those made in Pennsylvania.

This is hardly surprising, considering that many New Jersey girls crossed the Delaware River and attended schools in Philadelphia or the surrounding area. Patterns were certainly transported back and forth throughout the region, and in the process, trends in styles and colors developed and were copied across states and regions.

The visual presentation of New Jersey house samplers tends to be quite strong, making them good additions to a collection. They are easily found and vary in price from a few thousand dollars to tens of thousands, depending on the condition, and, especially, location. New Jersey pieces that originated in Burlington County are especially sought after by collectors and tend to be very expensive.

Mary Ann Hartshorne's Sampler, New Jersey, *c.*1810

Good color and graphic appeal make this sampler very collectible.

The diamond repeat border adds a nice edge to the sampler.

By placing her alphabets, worked in eyelet and cross-stitch, in the center, Mary made room for pictorial panels of flowers at the top and of house and landscape at the bottom.

Arched vines and leaves on either side of the house are a whimsical touch.

Size: 16¼ x 14½in/
41.2 x 36.8cm
Value: $3,000–4,000

▶ *Mary stitched a very appealing silk on linen sampler with a house and addition. Her inscription is a simple one:* Mary Ann Hartshorne's work aged 10 years when this was/ done.

Sarah Van Cleef's Sampler, New Jersey, 1811

In excellent condition with bold presentation, this sampler gets high marks with collectors.

Sarah added interest to her flower and bird panel by interspersing small birds, designs, and hearts throughout.

Sarah, unlike Mary, included the name of her teacher on her bright needlework.

The house includes wonderful detail, with the fenced roof, six chimneys, and checkered door-tops.

Size: 18¼ x 17¾in/
46.3 x 45cm
Value: $18,000–20,000

▶ Sarah gave her bold, silk on linen sampler an unusual manor house with wing additions. Sarah was born in Middlebush, Somerset, NJ. Her inscription indicates that the sampler was: . . . made under the care of/ mary bellamy.

▶ The checked panels above the door of Sarah's house are an unusual touch, and the roof appears to hold a widow's walk between the two chimneys. With windows that are neatly outlined and balanced, the whole effect is quite pleasing.

New Jersey Floral Samplers

The floral border samplers of New Jersey, worked in the late 18th and early 19th centuries, differ from those of New England and are easily identified. Several New Jersey schools produced samplers with distinctive designs. Eliza Rue's School in Pennington, NJ, characteristically included a two-color meandering vine with grape leaves and fruit. In many examples, a basket overflowing with flowers anchors the bottom portion of the sampler; a verse is usually stitched within the grape border.

Samplers made in Burlington County, NJ, are easily identified by their entwined, double-vine, meandering rose or floral border, like the one surrounding the sampler opposite. Center motifs on these samplers often include a building or house—in particular, the Westtown School of Chester County, PA—or a landscape scene. The samplers were produced at several different Quaker schools, and most include Quaker designs as fill-in motifs. Quaker school floral samplers are the largest identifiable group from New Jersey; important pieces bring very high prices.

New Jersey floral samplers are very appealing—large, quite pictorial, and beautiful to display, making them all the more appealing. Advanced collectors usually prefer the samplers exhibiting the Westtown School building over those with floral or unidentified house centerpieces. Although some pieces command remarkably high prices, many—like the examples shown on these pages—can be acquired for much less.

Maria Bake's Sampler, New Jersey, 1829

The grapevine border is typical of Eliza Rue's school. The two-tone leaves and vine create excellent contrast.

Maria stitched a quite popular verse, calling it an extract.

The large, overflowing basket is beautifully worked, providing a lovely focal point for the needlework.

From the collection of Joan Stephens, this piece sold at Sotheby's in 1997 for two and a half times the price Mrs. Stephens paid for it in 1988.

Size: 16 x 17in/
40.6 x 43.1cm
Value: $14,000–16,000

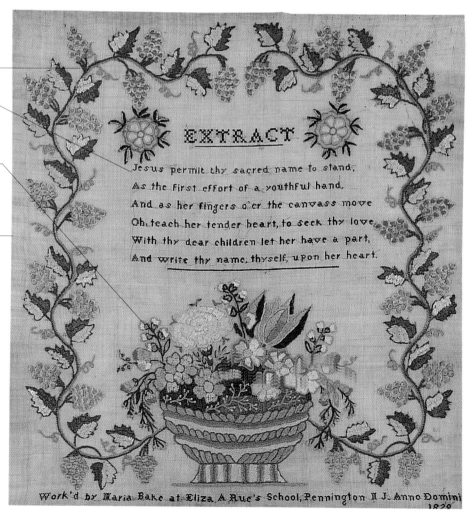

▶ Maria Bake was the daughter of Pierson and Hannah Eccles Bake of Pennington. She was born in 1813, married Woolsey Blackwell in 1839, and had three children. She died in 1890. Her silk on linen sampler identifies her school.

Susannah Thomas's Sampler, New Jersey, 1818

The double-vine rose border typifies pieces worked in Burlington County.

Susannah stitched the most common verse, but altered some of the wording: for example, "gracious" or "sacred" became "glorious," and "her" changed to a personal "my."

She included a large basket of flowers, as well as a tightly stitched, pictorial rural scene at the bottom.

Excellent color and condition make this sampler highly desirable.

Size: 20⁷/₈ x 23³/₄ in/
53 x 60.3cm
Value: $15,000–18,000

▶ Susannah was born in 1806 the daughter of Mr. (?) and Mary Steward Thomas. She inscribed her silk on linen sampler in this way: Susannah Steward Thomas aged 12 years/ Jesus permit thy glorious name to stand/ As the first efforts of an infant hand/ And while my fingers o'er this canvass move/ Engage my tender heart to feel thy love.

▶ Notice in this detail the closely worked pictorial scene Susannah stitched on the bottom of her sampler (above). The rural setting with house and church represents an idyllic landscape. She used contrasting colors to delineate windows, roofs, and other details.

New Jersey Pictorial Samplers

Samplers with scenic panels are the most visually graphic group from New Jersey. They exist in great numbers with many regional characteristics. The most highly prized come from the Burlington County area and feature the Westtown School in West Chester, PA. These generally large pieces show the school squarely set on a lawn scattered with animals. They also feature many Quaker motifs, a typical double-vine floral border, and a circular cartouche containing pertinent inscriptions.

Many schoolmistresses developed their own signature styles through pictorial designs worked in thread that their students would then replicate. One group of samplers from Burlington County features a large farm scene with a young woman on horseback; there are no alphabets or verse, and the only lettering is the name of the maker, stitched at the top. These pieces date from before 1810—earlier than most of the pictorial samplers from New Jersey, which date from the 1820s.

One small group of identified samplers were made at Mrs. E. Brown's Wesleyan Seminary. Two known pieces exist and are pictured on these pages, dated 1828 and 1829. Remarkably similar in composition, they nonetheless exhibit individual differences. This type of sampler was not a beginner's project, but rather the work of a more advanced needlework student.

A word of caution to the collector: because of the proximity to Pennsylvania, many girls from southern New Jersey attended school in Philadelphia and surrounding areas. The beautiful samplers they brought home were sometimes the basis for New Jersey samplers. Genealogies can be helpful in locating origin, but not always.

As with all samplers, condition is of the utmost importance in determining value. As we see here, Maria Furrer's work has survived in far better condition than that of Eliza Ann Newman. Because of their pictorial impact, both of these works make a fine addition to any collection.

Eliza Ann Newman's Sampler, New Jersey, 1828

Fading and acidic staining from the backing materials greatly diminish the value of this piece.

The girl in the window is a charming detail. She appears to be looking down on the figure in white.

The three-story house with double-doors has opened and closed shutters.

The little blue house to the right is two-story in this sampler and three-story in Maria's opposite.

Figures stitched in back of the fence add depth and are proportionate, while the large pot of flowers seems almost an afterthought with its disproportionate size.

Size: 16½ x 22in/
41.9 x 55.8cm
Value: $10,000–12,000

Maria S. Furrer's Sampler, New Jersey, 1829

Maria's design, with many of the same elements, creates visual interest by reversing some of the images.

Maria included not only her teacher's name in her inscription, but also the name of the school.

The checkered walks, doorway, and lampposts are nicely developed in Maria's sampler.

The colors are strong and the background remains unstained, making a very strong contrast.

The overall condition of this work is far superior to that of Eliza Ann's.

Size: 15¹/₂ x 16³/₄in/
39.3 x 42.5cm
Value: $18,000+

▶ Maria included five figures on her silk on linen sampler, as did Eliza Ann (opposite). But Maria placed them differently. The girl in the window is now behind the fence, while the woman in white appears to be walking to the blue house with a gentleman. These may be two interpretations of a wedding scene.

◀ Eliza Ann stitched a border of flowers on a thick vine on each side of her silk on linen sampler. This type of border is sometimes found on samplers from Chester County, PA.

◀ As seen in this detail, a pair of quirky little figures that Maria stitched on her sampler (above) appear almost cartoon-like. Samplers often represented a story line. In this case, the figure may be the daughter leaving her family home, marrying, and going to her new home with her husband.

New York Biblical Samplers

New York samplers based on biblical stories comprise the most enduring type of sampler made in America. Needleworkers first began stitching these samplers in the 1740s, and continued to produce them into the 1830s. Research suggests that samplers with a biblical theme were first worked at one of the French schools in New Rochelle, NY.

The format for this large group is based on bands. Each band features several biblical stories and scenes. Among the most popular of the stitched Bible stories were Adam and Eve in the Garden of Eden, Moses receiving the tablets of the Ten Commandments, Jacob and his dream-ladder to heaven, the near-sacrifice of Isaac, the New Testament parable of the sower, and Christ feeding the multitudes with fishes and bread. It is thought that many of these Bible motifs were copied from Dutch

tiles, which were also used to help teach Bible stories to young children.

Early biblical samplers from New York were bordered with geometric, three-leafed flowers or a strawberry border. They were often solidly stitched over the ground fabric so that the background did not show through. It is not uncommon to find later examples that were worked on a larger scale and do not have borders.

Figures are always desirable on samplers, creating visual appeal and drawing collector attention. Obviously, figures abound on the biblical samplers, and a few excellent examples exist that contain more than 25 figures and numerous animals. Highly collected, biblical samplers are not common, in spite of the long period during which they were stitched. Collectors should look for pieces that contain several different scenes.

Ann Yates's Sampler, New York, c.1785

Ann's inscription lines in the top and bottom bands are not finished.

The pictorial elements on this piece are well-stitched.

The center building seen here is found on many New York biblical samplers and may depict a church.

Color and condition here are excellent, but the unfinished areas decrease the value.

Size: 15⁵/₈ x 19¹/₈in/
39.6 x 48.5cm
Value: $8,000–10,000

Susannah Williams's Sampler, New York, 1830

Alphabets were not usually found on earlier pieces. These are in a 19th-century style.

The lack of border surround is typical of later samplers from this group.

Fiber loss in the lower alphabet does affect the price.

Excellent color and design make this sampler a good addition to a collection.

Although her work is larger and produced later than Ann's, Susannah's bands of pictorial work are almost identical to Ann's.

Size: 20¼ x 19⅛in/
51.4 x 48.5cm
Value: $15,000–18,000

▶ *Susannah's silk on linen sampler is one of the largest from this long-enduring group.*

◀ *Historical records have been found for two Ann Yates, one born in 1768 and one in 1772; both were christened at the First Dutch Reformed Church in Albany, NY. One of them presumably worked this silk on linen piece.*

▶ *The man-in-tree motif shown in this detail from the sampler above is found in abundance on New York biblical samplers. The man sometimes appears alone, and sometimes accompanied by a figure standing to the side, as here. It is thought that this figure might represent England's Charles II, hiding in the oak tree.*

New York House and Figure Samplers

In the first quarter of the 19th century, many girls made samplers in New York that to some extent recall those stitched in Massachusetts. It is possible that these patterns were carried to New York State by teachers migrating westward. Or it may be that students attending Eastern schools returned home with samplers they had made while there. These New York samplers bear an especially strong similarity to samplers made in Middlesex County, MA, and are therefore frequently confused.

The New York samplers are often stitched with three-sided borders of floral or geometric design. They sometimes include a cartouche at the bottom that encloses a name and other pertinent information. The center panel is typically composed of alphabets and numbers, sometimes including a verse, and followed by a panel with house, tree, and figures. Fortunately, many of the sampler makers inscribed their work with the place of origin, so the samplers can be identified accurately.

These pieces are almost always large and decorative, with an engaging, figured panel at the bottom. They make a nice addition to a collection and can be purchased at a reasonable price.

Lydia Weaver's Sampler, New York, 1809

The geometric border is quite unusual and decorative.

Little square boxes such as these are also found on samplers from Middlesex County, MA.

The large alphabet is separated from other motifs and is worked in eyelet stitch.

Lydia added charm to her work by stitching one figure—possibly meant to represent herself—with tree, pot of flowers, house, and bird, all in disproportion.

Although the colors are somewhat muted, the overall condition is excellent.

Size: 22½ x 16⅜in/
55.8 x 41.6cm
Value: $4,000–5,000

▶ *Lydia stitched this silk on linen sampler on a large scale and included her name, age, and location within the cartouche:* Lydia Weaver's work wrought in the 11th year of her age/ Troy in the year of our Lord 1809.

Melinda Borden's Sampler, New York, 1814

Melinda's border is light and airy. She repeated the pattern above the inscription line and on each side of the house.

In the pictorial panel, two figures approach a grand house that has large windows and an elaborate door.

The background fabric is an unbleached linen and loosely woven, allowing the backboard to show through the weave. A darker color backboard would unite the piece's overall color.

Charming samplers like this are much sought-after and should be reasonably priced, as they are not from a well-known or documented school.

Size: approx. 18 x 16½in/
45.7 x 41.9cm
Value: $5,000–6,000

▶ *Melinda's silk on linen sampler is similar in format to the one opposite and from the same town:* Melinda Borden Wrought This in the 10th/ year of her age 1814 Troy October.

▶ *This detail shows the elegant two-story, center-hall house with large paned windows Melissa worked on her sampler (above). She placed formal gardens in front of an unusual doorway. Her two female figures, out of proportion to either house or anatomy, have a folky look.*

New York Female Association School Samplers

In 1798, a group of Quaker women began the "Female Association" as a relief agency for the sick and poor in New York City. In 1801, the women branched out to open a school for both boys and girls. They soon limited the enrollment to female students. Needlework was an intrinsic part of the girls' instruction, and the students were encouraged to make samplers as gifts for members of the "Female Association." Over time, more Association schools were opened, and as they increased in number, the students would include a signature inscription that indicated, among other things, which school they were attending when they stitched the sampler.

The designs on these samplers followed a basic Quaker style. The girls stitched a central leaf cartouche containing alphabet, verse, and/or inscription. They further adorned their samplers with a variety of Quaker motifs, such as baskets, rose buds, and floral sprigs.

Because the samplers were intended as gifts, these pieces are usually rather small and include the maker's name and age, as well as the name of the Association member for whom the gift was created. Stitched in silk on linen of either a fine gauze or heavier weave, these samplers are an elaborate form of marking samplers and are in high demand.

Jane Vermilya's Sampler, New York, 1823

This sampler is not as vibrant as the piece opposite.

The large sprigs of flowers in the corners help to create a contrast to the blank linen.

Jane included a typical Quaker alphabet, a script alphabet, numbers, and a verse, followed by another two alphabets—all within her leaf cartouche.

Good color and more-than-average inscription make this a nice addition for collectors.

The Female Association School Number 3, referred to in Jane's inscription, opened in January 1815.

Size: 17in/43.1cm sq
Value: $2,500–3,500

Eliza McMannus's Sampler, New York, 1813

This is the earliest known Female Association School sampler. Eliza did not include a school number, so it is probable that it was made at the first school.

This small piece retains vivid color and excellent composition.

The rosebud motifs are quite typical of Quaker work.

From the collection of Joan Stephens, this sampler doubled in value from the time of its purchase in 1993 until its sale in 1997 at Sotheby's.

Size: 7 x 8in/17.7 x 20.3cm
Value: $18,000–20,000

▶ Evidently, Eliza stitched this silk on linen sampler as a gift for Mary Thompson to give to Elizabeth Thompson, as she inscribes: Eliza McMannus, aged 10 years./ Female Afsociation School, N.Y./ December 1813/ From Mary Thompson,/ a member of the Female/ Association,/ to Elizabeth Thompson.

◀ Jane stitched a larger than usual silk on linen sampler as a gift for her sponsor, Mary Collins. Jane's inscription gives ample information: Worked by/ Jane Vermilya aged/ 14 Years February/ 21st 1823 Female/ Association School/ No. 3/ For Mary D. Collins/ a member of the New/ York Female Association/ Could I by bearing Mary's name/ Like her be wise at heart,/ I might life's needless cares disclaim/ And choose her better part.

◀ This detail of Eliza's sampler (above) shows her distinctive treatment of the rosebud motif. This was a particularly popular element of Quaker samplers, which typically included profuse flowers. Eliza made it distinctive through her use of strong colors. In fact, Eliza's work is visually brighter and more appealing than many Quaker samplers, which were often worked in monochromatic silks.

New York Pictorial and Record Samplers

For some unknown reason, family records were not as popular a sampler form in New York State as they were in other regions, which is to say that not as many were produced. Those that do exist seem to be renditions of a sampler that was viewed elsewhere and simply copied. Without genealogical information, it can be difficult to impossible to attribute family records to New York; at the same time, it is possible that many New York records have been misidentified. The Bardeen Family Record pictured below is unusually late and most likely not the product of schoolwork, but rather a piece worked at home. The maker of this sampler would appear to have been not particularly well-educated.

Pictorial samplers, on the other hand, became a prevalent sampler style in the second quarter of the 19th century in New York. Many of these pieces were worked in small towns and depict local scenes, houses, and buildings. Often they do not include alphabets or verses; many are not signed in any way. They usually have a four-sided border framing the interior, giving them a decidedly picture-like quality.

Attribution to specific schools is not possible with these samplers, and unlike New York biblical samplers or those from the Female Association Schools, they do not command high prices. Collectors can find many fine pieces available for purchase from this region.

Bardeen Family Record, New York, c.1870

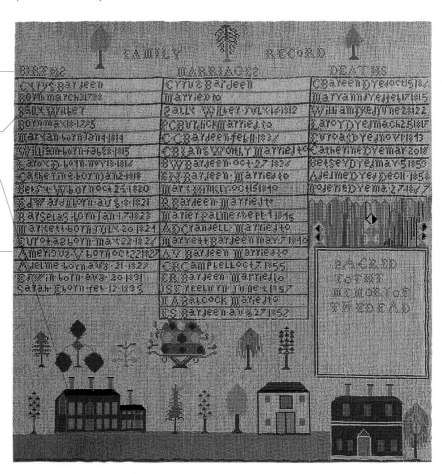

Chemical-dyed wool yarn, such as used here, became popular after the mid 1800s, replacing silk floss as the thread of choice.

The maker of this needlework probably had limited schooling, as she rendered many of her letters in reverse.

The buildings most likely represent those inhabited by family members.

Attractive and in good condition, this sampler provides an interesting genealogy, but samplers of this type are not very popular among collectors.

Size: 25in/63.5cm
Value: $4,000–5,000

▶ This unusual family record in wool on linen lists the births, marriages, and deaths of members of the Bardeen family. Cyrus was listed as a clothier and farmer in the 1850 census of Brookfield. His granddaughter described him as tall, quiet, and dignified.

Anna Margaret Houghtaling's Sampler, New York, 1835

Anna's border is exceptionally pretty—light and airy—and frames the content well.

The church and house are most likely buildings familiar to her. The window detail provides visual interest.

Engaging details, such as the duck pond and the flowered arbor, make the picture fuller and more attractive.

The excellent condition and good color of this sampler will appeal to a collector.

The fact that the school is unknown will keep the price lower.

Size: 16in/40.6cm sq
Value: $4,500–5,500

▶ *At age 9, Anna stitched a silk on linen village scene with house, church, and strolling figure. Her inscription indicates that she lived in Kingston.*

▶ *The detailing of Anna's duck pond and arbor in the sampler above is almost lost at first glance, because the buildings are large and prominent. Seen in this close-up, it becomes apparent that Anna's attention to detail here adds richness and interest to the overall picture.*

Pennsylvania German Marking Samplers

The samplers stitched by Pennsylvania German girls have many of the characteristics of those made in their homeland. The education of young women was not prevalent within this group of diverse religious sects until later in the 18th century. Before that time, girls were educated and taught needlework within the community by women who instructed them in familiar, longstanding traditions.

Sampler making had been included as part of a girl's education in both the Dutch and German cultures of Europe; it was continued in the rural Pennsylvania

settlements created by Dutch and German immigrants to North America. The marking samplers of the Pennsylvania German girls are often stitched in red and blue thread on a linen ground. The girls dotted their work with spot motifs of both Quaker and German design.

Usually small and very decorative, these samplers do not exist in great abundance but are nevertheless relatively inexpensive. Although not considered important pieces by advanced collectors, they have such charm, brightness, and primitive appeal as to make them nice additions for beginning sampler buyers.

Anonymous Sampler, Pennsylvania, c.1820

The format of this piece is unusual; it may have been intended as a book cover or cushion.

The building makes a good focal point for a sampler otherwise scattered with random motifs.

Bright color and unique design make this sampler more prized than the one opposite.

Size: 8 x 18in/
20.3 x 45.7cm
Value: $1,500–2,000

▲ *Although the linen on linen sampler above is unsigned, the maker reveals one fact of her life:* I have no Mother for she died/ When I was very young,/ But still her memory round my heart/ Like morning mists has hung.

▶ *This detail of the quaint piece above focuses on the unusual house and fenced yards. The latter may have been an orchard and a pen for animals. Typical of Pennsylvania sampler makers, the needleworker used red and blue to contrast strongly with a white linen ground.*

Bezette Risgeborenhorn's Sampler, Pennsylvania, *c.*1800

The irregular stitching and uneven lines indicate that this piece was probably made by a very young child.

Although the color is bright, ground fabric staining adversely affects the value.

Bezette's random motifs are typical of those found on German and Quaker samplers.

Size: approx. 8 x 11in/
20.3 x 27.9cm
Value: $800–1,200

▶ *Bezette created a brightly stitched linen on linen sampler that typifies Pennsylvania German style.*

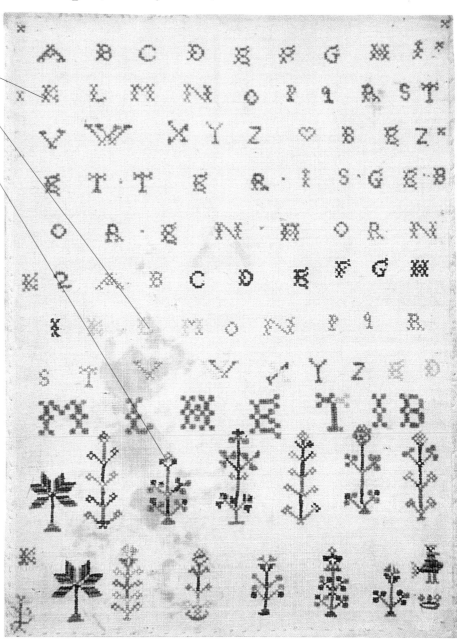

▼ *Notice in this detail how Bezette chose to incorporate her name into the design of her sampler (right). Rather than making it a separate design element, she embedded it between her two alphabets.*

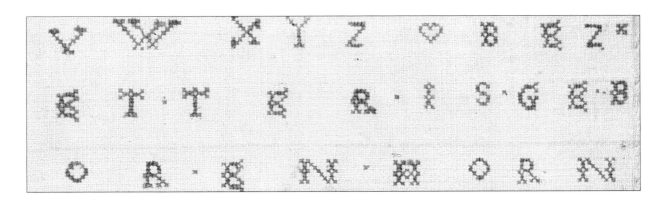

Pennsylvania
Philadelphia Samplers

Philadelphia girls produced a significant number of beautiful samplers in the 18th and 19th centuries. A large city for that era, Philadelphia had numerous schools and teachers, and consequently contributed many different sampler styles over the decades. Early work from the region tended to be English in style, with tight, banded patterns. By the beginning of the 19th century, however, the samplers had become larger and the motifs bolder. One of the more popular design elements was a house on a stepped terrace; this motif appeared in many variations throughout the Delaware Valley.

Large animals, birds and insects, baskets of flowers, and a bold strawberry border were all typical designs of the early 19th-century Philadelphia sampler. A sampler maker often included a floral cartouche encircling her name and the date of completion at the top of her extravagant work. Trees typically included weeping willows; a tree in a filled-in, upside-down heart shape; fruit trees of all sorts; and a strange, square tree worked in rows of solid stitching above a thin trunk.

Philadelphia samplers are very appealing. They are bold and dynamic and make attractive display pieces. When in excellent condition and from a noted school, they command high prices in today's marketplace. However, many Philadelphia samplers are found in only fair condition. In addition, many were made under the tutelage of an unidentified teacher. Samplers that are unidentified or in less than good condition can be acquired reasonably.

Eliza Sibbett's Sampler, Pennsylvania, *c.*1830

The cartouche held by angels is typical of a group of samplers from Philadelphia, *c.*1820–1835.

The large strawberry bands and floral borders worked through the center separate the motifs and prevent the designs from floating.

The well-developed house panel provides good visual focus and contains engaging detail on the buildings and yard.

If the school or teacher were known, the sampler would be worth considerably more.

Staining in the lower portion lessens the value.

Size: 24³⁄₈ x 21¹⁄₄ in/
61.9 x 53.9cm
Value: $12,000–15,000

Eliza Madara's Sampler, Pennsylvania, 1820

All of the elements in Eliza's sampler are unusually large.

The strong strawberry border with thin outer border is a good design that is not overpowered by the interior motifs.

The large flowers contain initials, probably those of her parents.

The deer eating grass adds a comical note.

The color is good, but water staining along the left side detracts from the value.

Size: 19³/₄ x 20¹/₄in/
50.1 x 51.4cm
Value: $18,000–20,000

▶ *Eliza Madara's large and folky silk on linen sampler is both charming and imaginative.*

◀ *Eliza Sibbett incorporated many designs on her large silk on linen needlework. It is unlikely she worked this at age eight; more likely, a numeral 1 was originally stitched in front of the 8, meaning she was 18 years old. It was not uncommon for a woman to pick out dates and numbers as she aged.*

▶ *This detail shows Eliza Sibbett's center-hall, two-story house, surrounded by a fenced dooryard garden where chicks peck for food. She included shuttered windows on her stone or brick building and added a string course to the masonry. The house dominates Eliza's sampler. The double-chimney building to the left appears to be the summer kitchen.*

Pennsylvania House Samplers

The houses and buildings pictured on Pennsylvania samplers are stitched in hundreds of styles and variations. The region's large size contributed to its comparatively diverse architecture. Samplers from this state depict many unique structures, most of which are quite unlike any found in New England.

Buildings did not generally appear on Pennsylvania samplers until the late 18th century; they became a dominant element in the 19th century. By then, band and lace samplers had long since gone out of style, and sampler composition had grown more fanciful and pictorial.

Sampler makers usually placed their houses at the bottom of the piece, within a landscape or alone, and usually with an alphabet section and possibly a verse above. Inscription lines became more involved, including not only the girl's name, but often her birth date and age and the town where the sampler was stitched. All of this data provides significant help to collectors. The more information available, the easier genealogical work becomes. Research sometimes results in finding the name of the schoolmistress—that is, the designer—the ultimate criterion for grouping samplers.

House samplers from Pennsylvania are plentiful. They vary in size, shape, regional origin, and price. They range as well from quite sophisticated to folky to plain. Inscribed information adds value, as do decorative motifs.

Fanny Keever, Pennsylvania, 1833

The alphabet is worked in eyelet stitch, and, between rows, Fanny stitched a number of unusual and decorative bands.

The border appears too small in proportion to the size of the sampler to be pleasing.

The overall good condition and the information given make this sampler desirable.

Fanny's building appears to be a Quaker meetinghouse, possibly the school she attended.

Size: 16½ x 13½in/
41.9 x 34.3cm
Value: $7,000–9,000

▶ *Fanny stitched a remarkably informative silk on linen sampler, with birth date, parents, and instructor. Fanny was born in Rafello Township, Lancaster County, PA.*

Sophia Fermoses, Pennsylvania, 1812

The double strawberry border with double flowers at the top is different from most borders.

Sophia's crooked lettering and spelling only add to the charm.

"In the 8 year" means that Sophia was seven when she stitched this work.

The two-chimney brick house with three-stories is an unusual style.

Small black dogs with curled up tails—common to English samplers—appear more on Pennsylvania samplers than on those of New England.

Sophia's complicated door treatment adds visual interest.

Size: 15½ x 17½in/
39.7 x 44.4cm
Value: $12,000–15,000

▶ Sophia was the daughter of George Fermoses, of the 6th Ward in Philadelphia. Her silk on linen sampler with silk ribbon border was probably made at a country or small day school and not at one of the prominent Philadelphia schools.

▶ Compare the two samplers' buildings, as seen in these close-ups. Fanny stitched an austere building (**near right**), probably a rendition of the Quaker school or meetinghouse. Sophia's house (**far right**) is a homey place, worked with uneven edges. Her skill with the needle at eight years of age cannot compare to Fanny's at 17.

Pennsylvania House Samplers—1830s and Later

Houses remained a popular sampler subject well into the 1830s and beyond. The format continued to resemble earlier 19th-century samplers, with alphabets covering several lines above a lower section devoted to scenes and decorative motifs—all surrounded by geometric or floral borders. The chief difference as the century progressed came down to the thread used to stitch the designs on the linen. Wool yarn, especially merino wool, became the choice of the day. Consequently, stitches became larger, and often a looser linen ground was employed as background material. The fineness of earlier samplers gave way to more elementary work.

While the teaching of sampler making continued in every girls' school curriculum in the 1830s and '40s, and the patterns used for samplers did not substantially change, the finished appearance of these pieces did. The bright colors, made possible by the advent of chemical dyes used

for wool yarn, made such yarn very attractive to stitchers, with the result that designs and the finished products tended to be much bolder and more colorful. At the same time, due to the larger size of wool yarn, the tiny details of earlier work were necessarily discarded, and the skills required to create such intricate effects lost.

In the collector's market, samplers dating from after 1850 are generally not grouped in the same category as schoolgirl needlework of earlier years. Samplers stitched in wool from the late 1820s through the 1840s, however, can often be attributed to specific schools and are still influenced by earlier sampler traditions. If not from a well-known and highly collected school, these wool-stitched samplers can be excellent buys for a collector. It is important to remember that not all wool-stitched samplers are American in origin; wool thread was popular in England and Scotland far earlier than in the United States.

Magdalene Binkly's Sampler, Pennsylvania, 1834

The bright colors here make the sampler visually appealing.

Thread loss throughout detracts from the piece's value.

Magdalene's inscription line shows damage, probably due to insect infestation, which was typical of samplers stitched with wool thread. Damage of any sort detracts from value.

Interestingly, Magdalene chose to change the border design she used on three sides when she worked the border at the bottom.

Size: 16¼in/41.2cm sq
Value: $1,500–2,000

Nancy Jane Fulton's Sampler, Pennsylvania, 1847

Graphically, this sampler is a visual delight, with a beautifully composed border and landscape and finely detailed elements.

The floral border is particularly well-developed for the period.

Nancy Jane continued a tradition by including the most popular sampler verse in her sampler.

The floral band creates a pleasing transition from the script to the picture portion of the sampler.

Size: 18 x 21in/45.7 x 53.3cm
Value: $14,000–16,000

▶ *Like Mary E. Ford (see page 87) 11 years earlier, Nancy Jane included this popular verse in her sampler of wool and cotton on linen:* Jesus permit thy gracious name to stand,/ As the first effort of a feeble hand:/ And while her fingers oe'r the canvas move,/ Engage her youthful heart to seek thy love:/ With thy dear children let her share a part,/ And write thy name thyself upon her heart *This sampler is elaborate for its period, with an intricately worked border and bottom pictorial panel.*

◀ *In this wool on linen sampler, Magdalene Binkly stitched several alphabets, numbers, and initials in the top portion of her sampler, then filled in the space below with numerous designs.*

Dyestuffs and Samplers

Until the 19th century, the dyes used for coloring textiles were derived from plants, shells, and insects. All yarn colors—whether in wool, cotton, linen, or silk—came from natural dyes. These dyes were surprisingly bright and colorfast, as is evident in much of the needlework that has come down to us.

Producing textile dyes involved planting, growing, and harvesting the dye sources, and then processing them by soaking, boiling, and straining to extract the dye. The process was tedious and smelly for indigo blue, as strong urine was used to set the dye.

Wool absorbed the dye more easily than did silk. As a result, dyers achieved stronger hues in the wool lots, as compared to the subtler shades of dyed silk. Much of the wool yarn was dyed at home and used for clothing, crewel embroidery, and household textiles. Sampler makers favored silk thread, which was imported, spun, and dyed, from England and the Far East.

Chemical dyes did not appear until the late 18th century. The earliest of these, "Turkey red," originated in the Far East, then traveled to the Continent, and finally to the United States in 1829. Other chemical dyes followed, and, by the 1850s, aniline dyes became the standard, largely relegating natural dyes to the past.

These dyes produced stronger, deeper colors and shades not found in natural sources. Bright shades of orange and purple in wool yarns are sure-signs that chemical, rather than natural dyes, were used.

Pennsylvania Quaker Samplers

The Quakers had long been established in Pennsylvania by the early 19th century. William Penn, the colony's founder, was awarded the land in the late 17th century by England's King Charles II as payment for a debt owed his father, Adm. William Penn. The land grant also served to rid England of someone King Charles II considered a religious fanatic. Displaying a modesty typical of the Quakers, William Penn objected when the king announced that he would name the new land Pennsylvania. After protesting that he did not want the notoriety, Penn was informed that the territory was not being named for him, "silly fellow," but rather for his father, the Admiral.

Quaker schools were well-known in England and soon became popular in Pennsylvania and the Delaware Valley. Many of the sampler designs that emanated from this region are almost exact copies of those worked at the Ackworth School in England. Many of the teachers at the famous Westtown School in Chester County, PA, had been students from that school.

The motifs stitched on Quaker samplers are relatively simple and the colors, usually subdued. Design elements include half-medallions, rosebuds, baskets of flowers, facing birds, and roman alphabets. Simple borders, circular cartouches, and initials also typify this group.

Many Quaker samplers are available for purchase today. Collectors should beware, however, of the similarity between samplers worked at the Westtown School in Pennsylvania and those worked in Ackworth, England. The latter tend to be quite a bit larger than the American Quaker pieces. Samplers from Westtown and other Quaker schools make lovely additions to a collection.

Sarah Leedom's Sampler, Pennsylvania, 1823

Sarah's large roman alphabet is very dramatic and bold.

Sarah scattered initials of her family throughout the sampler.

She included such typical motifs as facing birds, rosebuds, a basket of flowers, and medallions.

The simple border with bell flowers is dramatic, creating a nice edge to this rather plain sampler.

Size: 18¹⁄₂ x 15¹⁄₂in/
46.9 x 39.3cm
Value: $4,500–5,500

▶ *Sarah and her brothers all attended the Westtown Quaker School. Her silk on linen sampler was certainly executed there.*

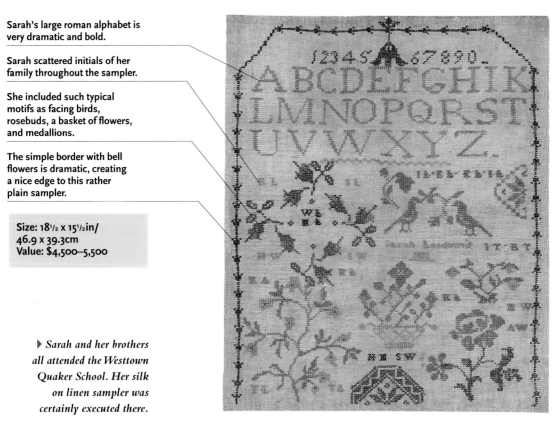

Elizabeth Trcziyulny's Sampler, Pennsylvania, *c.*1820

Elizabeth stitched a magnificent sampler with a bold and colorful design.

The separated large motifs are typically Quaker in design and indicate that Elizabeth probably attended a Quaker school.

The beehive creates a central focus, which Elizabeth has framed with the other elements.

The circular cartouche with facing birds nicely balances the house, beehive, and flowers.

This is an exceptional piece that commands an exceptional price.

Size: 19³/₈ x 19in/
49.2 x 48.2cm
Value: $18,000–20,000

▶ *Elizabeth's silk on linen sampler displays a much more complex design than the piece opposite, adding considerably to its value. Elizabeth is buried near State College, in central Pennsylvania.*

◀ *This detail from the sampler above shows the bee skep—a domed hive made of twisted straw—beautifully worked in crinkled silk and neatly placed on its platform in a garden setting. By using two contrasting colors, Elizabeth reproduced the look of a woven basket. The background willow was an excellent design choice and prevents the tan shades of the basket from falling immediately against the similar background color.*

Pennsylvania Compartmented Samplers

Compartmented samplers are an attractive group of samplers that were worked in the Susquehanna River Valley in the late 18th and early 19th centuries. Most likely an offshoot of earlier Philadelphia samplers, compartmented samplers feature various designs worked within boxed borders, or compartments, that form the edging of the sampler as well as elements within the body of the text.

Many of these samplers can be attributed to specific schools, among them that of Leah Bratten Galligher (later Leah Maguire). Her motifs of decorative boxes holding floral and geometric designs became popular throughout the area, and variations of her work prevailed for a considerable time. The central designs on these pieces are usually large pictorial scenes of couples in a landscape, women occupied with reading or handwork, or sometimes a religious theme such as Adam and Eve.

Stitched with silk yarns, the background fabric was either the typical medium-weight woven linen or a fine linen gauze. Often the sampler makers would edge their work with a silk ribbon or metallic thread lace.

Because of their visual appeal, these samplers are highly sought after, especially those naming Leah Galligher or Leah Maguire. Examples in good condition are relatively uncommon and can bring high sums. Those from other schools, while often equally appealing, are less costly.

Elizabeth Hoover's Sampler, Pennsylvania, 1803

Elizabeth named her teacher, a big plus in the sampler market.

The central picture here is charming, perhaps portraying Elizabeth herself.

Note the whimsical tree trunk with its climbing floral vines.

The compartments bordering three sides of the sampler are typical of Leah Bratten design. The heart is a common design element of many Lancaster County samplers.

The bottom panel is unusual with a half figure of a female.

Despite the strength of design and execution on this sampler, it loses a significant amount of value because of its stained and faded condition.

Size: 16¼ x 15⅛in/
41.2 x 38.4cm
Value: $8,000–10,000

Mary Eshelman's Sampler, Pennsylvania, 1822

The spelling is worked in the old style, using the letter "f" in place of "s"; many words are misspelled.

Isabella Sample, Mary's teacher and the designer of this sampler, used several of the elements found in Leah Maguire's designs.

Although writing dominates the interior of this work, Mary's use of color, attractive border, and large house makes for visual interest.

The floral side borders are unusual and provide a contrast to the angular designs of other elements.

The excellent condition and color of this piece contribute greatly to its value.

Size: 21in/53.3cm sq
Value: $18,000–20,000

▶ *Mary's cousin Ann made an identical sampler to this silk on linen piece in the same year. Mary inscribed her sampler this way:* **Mary Efhleman a Daughter Of John and/ Alice Efhelman waf born April 30 187 and/ Made Thif Sampler in The Year 1822 in/ Ifablla Samplef School.**

◀ *Elizabeth worked her sampler in silk, metal, and hair on a fine linen ground. She included a wealth of information, giving her name, age, date of birth, location, and teacher's name (Mrs. Leah Bratten).*

Leah Bratten Galligher Maguire

In 1800, Leah Bratten and her husband, Francis Galligher, placed a joint advertisement for a school. By 1802, their marriage was coming to an end. Francis ran an advertisement reading, "CAUTION," announcing that he was no longer responsible for Leah, for "she has absconded from my bed and board." Further accusations resulted in a public notice from Leah's brother George stating that they had "dissolved the bands of matrimony." It further accused Francis of unmanly conduct.

Leah moved to Harrisburg shortly thereafter and opened another school. In 1805, she married Isaac Maguire.

They had four children: John Bratten Armstrong (1806), William (1809), Sarah (1811), and Isaac (1812), the last when Leah was 48. The elder Isaac worked as a shoemaker, and Leah taught, while they raised their family. Historian William Henry Egle paints the picture of a fun-loving woman who sometimes wore outrageous costumes, played the fiddle, and enjoyed giving parties for her pupils. By contrast, Egle portrays Isaac as a quiet, submissive man giving way to all of Leah's whims.

Leah taught into the 1820s—the last known sampler naming her school is dated 1826. She died in 1830.

Pennsylvania Family Samplers

Occasionally, samplers turn up in pairs, sometimes stitched by the same girl, more often worked by sisters or cousins. In rare instances, mother and daughter, grandmother and granddaughter, or aunt and niece combinations appear. In these latter cases, much of the interest lies in seeing the older woman's work—executed when the woman was a girl herself—alongside that of her younger relative. The earlier pieces tend to be more intricate and detailed, and often, the stitching much finer, a clue to the evolution of needlecraft over the course of one or more generations.

The two examples illustrated here were worked by Eliza Yost and her niece Margaret Finkbeiner. Eliza stitched her piece in 1836; Margaret worked her sampler 26 years later, in 1862. Eliza's well-executed design indicates that she attended school, where she stitched her needlework in silk on a linen ground. Decades later, Margaret based her sampler on the work of her aunt, inscribing in pencil on the back of the piece "taught by Aunt Eliza Yost." She used cotton thread on a linen ground.

The earlier sampler at right is certainly the more elaborate. The border of large circular flowers frames the interior work. Decorative motifs surround and balance the verse and inscription, while the large basket of flowers centers the lower portion. In contrast, Margaret's sampler below has no border. Although she stitched several alphabets, she did not include a verse. And while she did copy her aunt's basket of flowers closely, as well as a few of the other elements, she did not achieve the dynamic graphic appeal of Eliza's work.

Margaret Finkbeiner's Sampler, Pennsylvania, 1862

Margaret did not balance her motifs in the lower portion of her sampler, favoring the right side.

Margaret's pot of flowers is almost exactly the same as the pot stitched on her aunt's sampler.

Cotton thread gives the sampler a flat look, as compared to the silk used by Eliza.

This sampler by itself would not have the collectible value it enjoys in combination with the sampler made by Eliza.

Size: 18 x 17in/45.7 x 43.1cm
Value: $7,000–9,000

▶ *Margaret stitched several motifs found on her Aunt Eliza's work, but omitted the border on her cotton on linen sampler.*

Eliza Yost's Sampler, Pennsylvania, 1836

The small pots of flowers seen here are typical of Philadelphia samplers.

Eliza leaves no doubt that this is her "Needle Work."

Eliza stitched an unusual, stylized pot of flowers, using geometric lines, squared-off leaves, and a large tulip that protrudes from the top.

Colorful and in excellent condition, this sampler has great collecting appeal.

Size: 21½ x 17¾in/
54.6 x 45cm
Value: $15,000–18,000

▶ *Eliza stitched a large sampler with a very bold border and inscribed it with name, date, and verse:* My youthful Labour of my Hands/ Here on this growing canvass stand/ Go view the Gardens And you'll see/ The (?) (?) Been by me/ Eliza Yost's/ Needle Work 1836.

▶ *In these details, note the subtle differences between the two girls' pots. Eliza's (far right) is worked with smaller stitches, and she spaced the diamond interior shapes better. Her tulip atop the arrangement is outlined with a dark color so that it stands out against the color of the linen, whereas Margaret's tulip (near right) blends into the background.*

Maryland and Delaware Marking Samplers

Samplers from Maryland and Delaware are not plentiful, which makes them quite a find for any collector. Maryland and Delaware girls did produce a significant group of "fruit and flower" pieces, but where exactly they were stitched remains a matter of speculation. More modest samplers can rarely be identified by design alone—they are sometimes confused with samplers of similar design from other regions, where they were made in great abundance.

The Quaker Boarding School in Wilmington, DE, produced a large number of samplers. The work stitched there is similar to that done in other Quaker schools—not surprising, given the movement of teachers within the system and the uniform instruction offered throughout. Many of these are "Extracts," stitched with black silk on fine linen. Alphabets, verse, and inscription were stitched within a meandering vine and leaf cartouche.

Other samplers stitched in country day schools throughout Maryland and Delaware seem simple and plain when compared to those created in the Quaker schools. Those that identify a place of origin are rare and therefore highly prized by collectors.

Mary Hargest's Sampler, Maryland, 1821

Mary separated each line with a row of decorative stitching, and surrounded the whole with a simple wave border.

Baltimore is boldly featured in the most prominent alphabet band worked in eyelet stitch.

Decorative detail would have enhanced the work.

Mary stitched two verses, four alphabets, numbers, and the date, January 23.

Good color and condition, along with date and important information, make this a highly collectible sampler.

Size: 16¼in/41.2cm sq
Value: $2,000–3,000

▶ Mary stitched this very large and colorful marking sampler in silk on linen. She included the much-prized location: **Mary Hargest Mark'd this in the 12th Year of her Age./ Baltimore 1821.**

Martha Newbold's Sampler, Delaware, 1818

The bold roman alphabet at the top is common to Quaker pieces.

Although there is some foxing to the background, the piece is in good overall condition.

Martha attributed her sampler to the Wilmington Quaker Boarding School, which opened in 1811, a plus for the piece's value.

This piece was once in the Joan Stephens collection, making it highly prized among collectors. In the 11 years from her purchase to its sale at auction, its value increased by over 1,000 percent.

Size: 11 x 13in/27.9 x 33cm
Value: $10,000–12,000

▶ *The meandering vine with four-sided leaves that Martha included on her silk on linen sampler originated at the Westtown School. It is typical of the cartouche border used on Quaker samplers both in Westtown, PA, and Wilmington, DE. In 1818, the Wilmington headmistress was from Westtown.*

▶ *This detail of Martha's sampler (above) shows the large, bold roman alphabet typical of Quaker samplers. The clean lines apparently made this lettering an appealing choice for the austere aesthetic of Quaker designs.*

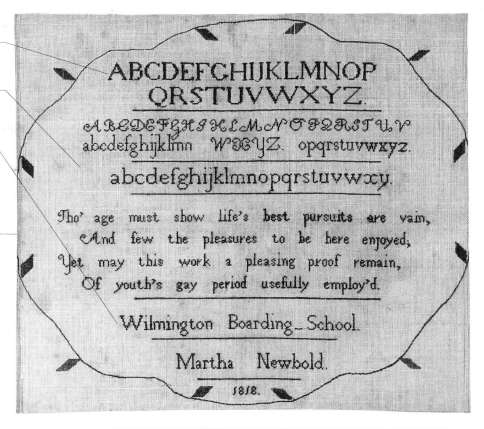

◀ *Notice in this detail how Mary worked time and date into the alphabet on her sampler (opposite), rather than setting them apart from the practice alphabets as Martha did above.*

Delaware House and Floral Samplers

Several distinct groups of samplers were created in Delaware. Some are quite similar in design to Pennsylvania and New Jersey pieces, with which they are often confused. Most impressive are the fruit and flower samplers, worked by girls from both Maryland and Delaware. The unusually wide borders of flowers, often topped with a large pineapple, are distinctive enough that they cannot be mistaken; and the fact that they can be attributed increases the prices they command. Other Delaware samplers, however, are less easy to identify.

The house sampler illustrated below is one of a small group of samplers made in Lewes, DE. Another, almost identical to this one was worked by Ellen Roades and is pictured in Betty Ring's *Girlhood Embroidery*. In the Roades piece, the main element is a two-story brick house with a gazebo and spindly pine trees to the side and a green lawn beneath all. The cartouche is a Quaker-like circle with facing birds; names and initials are scattered throughout.

Another Delaware sampler group features strong colors with a wide border of flower sprigs and large corner rosebuds and roses. The center portion is composed of colorful alphabets in bands above a verse and cartouche. These pieces are very dramatic and considered quite a prize when added to a collection.

Because Wilmington was home to several Quaker schools, many Wilmington samplers resemble those made in Philadelphia, where Quaker schools predominated. A knowledge of genealogy and a close study of samplers from both regions will help in identification.

Peggy West's Sampler, Delaware, 1808

The wide basket and floral border at the top and the hanging grapes at the side are typical of this sampler school.

The round cartouche with facing doves and inscription, "An Emblem of Innocence," typifies Quaker school motifs.

Peggy's house and gazebo (or perhaps outhouse) are well-proportioned with appealing detail.

The small stain in the lower left corner distracts somewhat, and the overall color is slightly faded; both affect the price.

The sampler falls into a highly sought category, and its general appearance is good.

Size: 17½in/44.4cm sq
Value: $6,000–8,000

Jane Wilson's Sampler, Delaware, 1791

The elaborate floral border is vivid and well designed. Note that not all of the floral sprigs are mirror images.

Colorful banding between the rows of alphabets makes the interior less monotonous.

The small corner rose next to the cartouche appears almost to be a signature.

This is a rare piece, in excellent condition and color.

Size: 14³/₄ x 12in/
37.4 x 30.4cm
Value: $20,000–30,000

▶ Jane, daughter of William and Rebecca Young Wilson of Mill Creek Hundred (northwest of Wilmington), was 13 years old when she stitched this silk on linen piece. She later married William Thomson, and they had eight children.

◀ Peggy's silk on linen work is almost identical to a sampler worked by Ellen Roades in the same year. The girls were classmates, and Peggy included her friend's name on her sampler.

◀ This detail from the sampler above shows Jane's skill as a needleworker. The rosebud in the neatly stitched border is well-executed and the rose, stylistically worked. The instructress who designed these patterns obviously had an artistic flair.

Virginia Samplers

In the South as in the North, sampler making was an important part of a girl's education. A girl's first sampler was a marking piece, such as the piece below, worked primarily to teach alphabets and the stitching skills needed to initial household textiles for identification.

Far fewer samplers have come to us, however, from states south of the Mason-Dixon Line than from those to the north of it. For one thing, the hot and humid weather of the South does not lend itself to cozy indoor activities like stitching samplers. That same weather is also not conducive to the preservation of delicate textiles. It weakens fabrics and gives rise to a large population of insects that feed on wool, cotton, and linen. Because of the scarcity of samplers, regional characteristics can be difficult to discern, and many samplers that may have been worked in the South are misidentified.

Nonetheless, Virginia samplers have come down to us, and they are eagerly sought after, especially by Southern collectors. While these pieces are difficult to categorize, and assigning specific characteristics to them can be problematic, recent research is helping to shed new light on this field. Today's collectors are much better able to assess Virginia samplers and acquire them knowledgeably. The work of Kimberly Smith Ivey at Colonial Williamsburg, especially, has helped identify many Southern schools and sampler groups.

Sidney Fitz Randolph's Marking Sampler, Virginia, c. 1820

The simplicity of Sidney's sampler and the monochromatic palette may indicate that it was stitched at an orphanage or small country school.

The dominant design feature of the sampler is its classic roman alphabet worked in a block stitch.

The bold roman alphabet is typical of the lettering style used on Quaker pieces.

The sampler is in good condition and contains more elements than the average marking piece, adding to its value.

Size: 15⁷/₈ x 12in/
40.3 x 30.4cm
Value: $2,000–3,000

▶ *Sidney Fitz Randolph is probably the name of a boy. It was not uncommon in small schools or orphan asylums for boys to learn needlework with the girls. Sidney produced this piece in silk on linen.*

Mary Ann Amanda Fall's Sampler, Virginia, 1839

Mary Ann incorporated several alphabets in different styles, increasing the value of the piece.

The bands that separate the alphabets add visual interest.

The small patch of flame stitch worked in the corner of this sampler is an unusual element for such a well-designed piece.

Note that the house panel displays numerous outbuildings in addition to the house itself.

Size: 17in/43.1cm sq
Value: $10,000–12,000

▷ *Mary Ann's silk on linen sampler is far more complicated and impressive than the other two shown here. The variety of elements, attention to detail, and fine needlework combine to make this piece extraordinary in both appeal and value.*

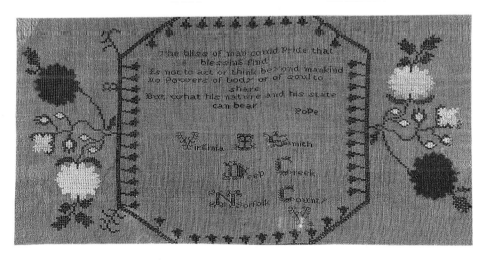

◁ *This silk on linen sampler by Virginia 1. Smith of Deep Creek, Norfolk County, VA, was stitched sometime in the 19th century. Because the sampler is small (approx. 7 × 12in/17.7 × 30.4cm) and relatively plain, it would probably sell for a tenth of what the sampler above could bring, despite the fact that the maker identified herself and her location.*

Washington, DC, Samplers

A small group of interesting samplers came from Washington, DC, and its surrounding areas, including Washington City, Georgetown, and Alexandria. Several schools and groups of samplers have been identified from this area; however, relatively few of the samplers have been accurately identified on the sampler market. Many resemble Philadelphia or Virginia samplers, and still others are so plain that they cannot be assigned to any particular area. Fortunately, there are some DC samplers available that were signed by the maker, dated, and identified according to place of origin.

Like their northern counterparts, most Washington, DC, samplers are worked with silk floss on a linen ground. A few known pieces were stitched on a green linsey-woolsey background. The marking samplers are quite hard to identify because of their simplicity and similarity to pieces made elsewhere in America. Easily identified samplers depict a large building, possibly a school, set on grass and identified as "Washington Navy Yard." Other common elements include triangular trees with birds perched on top, large baskets of flowers, brick houses and buildings, round and floral cartouches, and floral borders.

Because they are rare, these pieces are in great demand and often command prices higher than comparable samplers from other areas. A beginning collector should be careful about overpaying for a DC sampler, however, especially if similar samplers from other regions are available that are equal in quality and lower in price.

—G. Simmons's Sampler, Washington, DC, 1827

A neatly organized marking sampler, this piece offers decorative banding between the rows of alphabets.

The large basket gives the sampler a pleasing focal point.

Although more information is given and more decorative elements included than on the sampler opposite, the monochromatic color scheme detracts from the value of this piece.

Note that the first name of the maker has been either worn away or picked out.

Size: 16½ x 12⅜ in/
41.9 x 32cm
Value: $2,000-3,000

▶ The inscription on this silk on linen sampler offers scant but nonetheless valuable information, reading simply: —G. Simmons Work Washington City Oct. th 2d/ 1827.

Mary Ann Scott's Sampler, Washington, DC, 1831

From the former collection of Joan Stephens, this sampler nearly quintupled in value from the time of Stephens's purchase of it in 1993 to its sale at Sotheby's in January 1997.

The cartouche holding Mary Ann's name is unusual and elaborate compared to the rest of the work.

Mary Ann stitched a very solid-looking brick building with symmetrical trees on either side.

This may be a rendition of the Navy Yard school. Other renditions show a brick building with three shuttered windows on the second floor and one on either side of the door.

The small black dogs are quite common on British samplers, and at times cause misidentification.

Size: 20 x 17in/
50.8 x 43.1cm
Value: $8,000–10,000

▶ *Mary Ann's silk on linen sampler was exhibited at the Washington, DC, Antique Show in January 1989 and at the DAR Museum exhibition, "Magnificent Intentions," from September 1991 to March 1992. This was probably worked at Lydia English's Seminary in Georgetown—a Mary A. Scott, daughter of Joseph Scott, of Worcester County, PA, was registered there 1826–1831.*

◀ *The basket shown in this detail from the sampler above is filled to capacity. Although Mary Ann stitched a rather plain building with uneven bricks, she outdid herself when stitching the floral portion of her sampler. Close study can sometimes date a piece or locate its origin by the style of the baskets of floral bouquets.*

▶ *Sarah Crosby,*
Massachusetts, 1812.
Sarah stitched this floral
sampler "in the fourteenth
year of her age." The lovely
floral panel, worked in
crimped silk, distinguishes
this piece from the typical
alphabet marking sampler.
16³/₈ × 15in/1.6 x 38.1cm.

Sources & References

Where to See Samplers

The following is a list of museums and historical societies in which you will find collections of samplers, silk embroideries, and canvaswork pictures in your area. Such collections provide an excellent opportunity to become acquainted with different types and quality of samplers. Call in advance for exhibit information.

Antiques dealers who specialize in needlework may offer an excellent starting place when you're ready to start or add to your own collection. Watch your local papers, as well, for antique shows and fairs. These may offer the best opportunities for discovering a sampler that has just arrived in the collectibles market, whether from an estate sale, a small family collection, or simply someone's overloaded attic.

The Abby Aldrich Rockefeller Folk Art Center
Colonial Williamsburg
307 South England Street
Williamsburg, VA 23187
757-229-1000

American Folk Art Museum
45 West 53rd Street
New York, NY 10019
212-265-1040

Anglo-American Art Museum
Memorial Tower
Louisiana State University
Baton Rouge, LA 70803
504-388-4003

The Art Institute of Chicago
Department of Textiles
Michigan Avenue at Adams Street
Chicago, IL 60693
312-443-3696

Atlanta Historical Society
3099 Andrews Drive NW
Atlanta, GA 30305
404-233-2991

The Baltimore Museum of Art
Art Museum Drive
Baltimore, MD 21218
410-396-6266

Bayou Bend Collection of the Museum of Fine Arts
P.O. Box 13157, 1 Westcott Street
Houston, TX 77019
713-529-8773

Beverly Historical Society
117 Cabot Street
Beverly, MA 01915
617-922-1186

Camden County Historical Society
Park Boulevard and Euclid Avenue
Camden, NJ 08103
609-964-3333

Chester County Historical Society
225 North High Street
West Chester, PA 19380
215-696-4755

Chicago Historical Society
Clark Street at North Avenue
Chicago, IL 60201
312-642-4600

Cincinnati Art Museum
Art Museum Drive
Cincinnati, OH 45202
513-721-5204

Clara Barton House
5801 Oxford Road
Glen Echo, MD 20768
301-492-6246

Concord Antiquarian Society
200 Lexington Road
Concord, MA 01742
617-369-9609

Connecticut Historical Society
1 Elizabeth Street
Hartford, CT 06105
860-236-5621

Cooper-Hewitt Museum of Decorative Arts & Design
Smithsonian Institute
2 East 91st Street
New York, NY 10028
212-810-2011

Daughters of the American Revolution
1776 D Street NW
Washington, DC 20006
202-879-3241

Greenfield Village and Henry Ford Museum
20900 Oakwood Boulevard
Dearborn, MI
313-271-1620

The Henry Francis du Pont Winterthur Museum
Route 52, Kennett Pike
Wilmington, DE 19735
302-656-8591

The Heritage Center Museum
13 West King Street
Lancaster, PA 17603
717-299-6440

Historic Deerfield
Deerfield, MA 03421
413-774-5581

The Historic New Orleans Collection
533 Royal Street
New Orleans, LA 70130
504-523-7146

Stephen & Carol Huber
Sampler Gallery
40 Ferry Road
Old Saybrook, CT 06475
860-388-6809

Jefferson County Historical Society Museum
228 Washington
Watertown, NY 13601
315-782-3491

John Greenleaf Whittier Home
86 Friend Street
Amesbury, MA 01913
617-388-1337

Juliette Gordon Low Girl Scout National Center
142 Bull Street
(mail, 11 York Lane East)
Savannah, GA 331401
912-233-4501

Kent House State Commemorative Arts
P.O. Box 4354
Bayou Rapides Road
Alexandria, LA 71301
318-445-5611

Kentucky Museum
Western Kentucky University
Bowling Green, KY 42101
502-745-2592

Kentucky Historical Society Museums
Box H
Broadway at St. Clair Mall
Frankfort, KY 40601
502-564-3016

Lancaster County Historical Society
230 N. President Avenue
Lancaster, PA 17603
717-392-4633

Leffingwell Inn
348 Washington Street
Norwich, CT 06360
860-887-2506

Litchfield Historical Society
P.O. Box 385
Corner of South and East Streets
Litchfield, CT 06759
203-576-5862

Los Angeles County Museum of Art
5905 Wilshire Boulevard
Los Angeles, CA 90036
213-857-6083

Lyman Allen Museum
100 Mohegan Avenue
New London, CT 06320
860-443-2545

Maine Historical Society
485 Congress Street
Portland, ME 04111
207-774-1822

Marblehead Historical Society
The Jeremiah Lee Mansion
161 Washington Street
Marblehead, MA 01945
617-631-1069

Maryland Historical Society
201 West Monument Street
Baltimore, MD 21201
410-685-3750

Mercer Museum of the Bucks County Historical Society
Pine and Ashland Streets
Doylestown, PA 18901
215-345-0210

The Metropolitan Museum of Art
American Decorative Arts
  Department
Fifth Avenue at 82nd Street
New York, NY 10028
212-879-5500

Minneapolis Institute of Arts
2400 Third Avenue South
Minneapolis, MN 55405
612-870-3102

Moravian Museum of Bethlehem
66 West Church Street
Bethlehem, PA 18018
215-867-0173

Museum of the City of New York
Fifth Avenue at 103rd Street
New York, NY 10029
212-534-1672

Museum at Stony Brook
Route 5A
Stony Brook, NY 11790
516-751-0066

Museum of Early Southern Decorative Arts
924 South Main Street
Winston-Salem, NC 27108
919-722-6148

Museum of Fine Arts
Department of Textiles
465 Huntington Avenue
Boston, MA 02115
617-267-9300

Museum of International Folk Art
Museum of New Mexico
706 Camino Lejo
Santa Fe, NM 87504
505-827-8350

Nantucket Historical Association
Fair Street
Nantucket, MA 02554
617-228-1538

National Museum of American History
Division of Textiles
Smithsonian Institution
Constitution Avenue
Washington, DC 20560
202-357-1889

The Nevada State Museum
600 N. Carson Street
Capitol Complex
Carson City, NV 89710
702-885-4810

New Hampshire Historical Society
30 Park Street
Concord, NH 03301
603-225-3381

The New Jersey Historical Society
230 Broadway
Newark, NJ 07104
201-483-3939

New Jersey State Museum
P.O. Box 1868, 205 W. State Street
Trenton, NJ 08625
609-292-5420

The New York Historical Society
170 Central Park West
New York, NY 10024
212-873-3400

New York State Historical Association
Fenimore House
Lake Road
Cooperstown, NY 13326
607-547-1400

Newport Historical Society
82 Touro Street
Newport, RI 02840
401-846-0813

North Andover Historical Society Headquarters
153 Academy Road
North Andover, MA 01845
617-686-4035

Old Gaol Museum and Emerson-Wilcox House
Route 1A
York, ME 03909
207-363-3872

Old Sturbridge Village
1 Old Sturbridge Village Road
Sturbridge, MA 01566
508-347-3362

Old Washington, Inc.
P.O. Box 225, Main Street
Washington, KY 41096
606-759-7431

Peabody Essex Museum of Salem
161 Essex Street
Salem, MA 01970
617-745-1876

Philadelphia Museum of Art
Parkway at 26th Street
Philadelphia, PA 19101
215-787-5404

Plymouth Antiquarian Society
27 North Street
Plymouth, MA 02360
617-746-0012

Rhode Island Historical Society
John Brown House
52 Power Street
Providence, RI 02906
401-331-8575

Schenectady County Historical Society
32 Washington Avenue
Schenectady, NY 12305
518-374-0863

Society for the Preservation of New England Antiquities
141 Cambridge Street
Boston, MA 02114
617-227-3956

The St. Louis Art Museum
Forest Park
St. Louis, MO 63110
314-721-0067

Strawberry Banke, Inc.
P.O. Box 300
Hancock and Washington Streets
Portsmouth, NH 03801

Valentine Museum
1015 W. Clay Street
Richmond, VA 23219
804-649-0711

Warren County Historical Society Museum
P.O. Box 223, 105 S. Broadway
Lebanon, OH 45036
513-932-1817

Wilton Historical Society
249 Danbury Road
Wilton, CT 06897
203-762-7257

Woodlawn Plantation
P.O. Box 37
Mount Vernon, VA 22121
703-780-3118

The American Museum in Britain
Claverton Manor
Bath BA2 7BD
UK

The Fitzwilliam Museum
Trumpington Street
Cambridge CB2 1RB
UK

Victoria & Albert Museum
Cromwell Road
London SW7 2RL
UK

Royal Ontario Museum
100 Queen's Park
Toronto, Ontario M5S 2C6
Canada

Museum for Textiles
55 Centre Avenue
Toronto, Ontario M5G 2H5
Canada

Other Sources of Information

Allen, Gloria Seaman. *Family Record Genealogical Watercolors and Needlework.* Washington, DC: DAR Museum, 1989.

Ashton, Leigh. *Samplers, Selected and Described.* London, England, and Boston, MA: The Medici Society, 1926.

Bolton, Ethel Stanwood, and Coe, Eve Johnston. *American Samplers.* Boston, MA: The Massachusetts Society of the Colonial Dames of America, 1921.

Brown, Clare, and Wearden, Jennifer. *Samplers from the Victoria and Albert Museum.* London, England: V & A Publications, 1999.

Colby, Averil. *Samplers.* London, England: B.T. Batsford, 1964.

Conant, Rita F., and LaBranche, John F. *In Female Worth and Elegance: Sampler and Needlework Students and Teachers in Portsmouth, New Hampshire 1741–1840.* Portsmouth, NH: The Portsmouth Marine Society, 1996.

Davidson, Mary M. *Plimoth Colony Samplers.* Marion, MA: The Channings, 1974.

Edmonds, Mary Jaene. *Samplers and Samplermakers: An American Schoolgirl Art 1700–1850.* New York, NY: Rizzoli, 1991.

English Samplers at the Fitzwilliam. Cambridge, England: Fitzwilliam Museum, 1984.

Epstein, Kathleen. *British Embroidery and Curious Works from the Seventeenth Century.* Austin, TX: Curious Works Press, 1998.

Epstein, Kathleen. *Samplers in the European Tradition.* Austin, TX: Curious Works Press, 2000.

Fawdry, Marguerite, and Brown, Deborah. *The Book of Samplers.* New York, NY: St. Martin's Press, 1980.

Graffam, Olive Blair. "Youth is the Time for Progress," *The Importance of American Schoolgirl Art 1780–1860.* Washington DC: DAR Museum, 1998.

Hersh, Tandy and Charles. *Samplers of the Pennsylvania Germans.* Birdsboro, PA: Pennsylvania German Society, 1991.

Hornor, Marianna Merritt. *The Story of Samplers.* Philadelphia, PA: Philadelphia Museum of Art, 1971.

Huish, Marcus. *Samplers and Tapestry Embroideries.* Second edition. London, England: Longmans, Green, and Co., 1913.

Humphrey, Carol. *Samplers.* Fitzwilliam Museum Handbooks. Cambridge, England: Cambridge University Press, 1991.

Jones, Mary Eirwen. *British Samplers.* Oxford, England: Pen-in-Hand Publishing Co., 1948.

Ivey, Kimberly Smith. *In the Neatest Manner: The Making of the Virginia Sampler Tradition.* Colonial Williamsburg and Curious Works Press, 1997.

King, Donald. *Samplers.* London, England: Crown Publishers, 1960.

Krueger, Glee F.A. *Gallery of American Samplers: The Theodore H. Kapnek Collection.* New York, NY: E.P. Dutton, 1978.

Krueger, Glee F. *New England Samplers to 1840.* Sturbridge, MA: Old Sturbridge Village, 1978.

Parmal, Pamela. *Samplers from A to Z.* Boston, MA: MFA Publications, 2000.

Phelan, Dorothy Bromiley. *The Point of the Needle: Five Centuries of Samplers and Embroideries.* Greenville, SC: Curious Works Press, 2001; also, Stanbridge, Dorset, England: The Dovecote Press Ltd., 2001.

Ring, Betty. *American Needlework Treasures.* New York, NY: E.P. Dutton, 1987.

Ring, Betty. *Girlhood Embroidery: American Samplers & Pictorial Needlework, 1650–1850.* New York, NY: Knopf, 1993.

Ring, Betty. *Let Virtue Be a Guide to Thee: Needlework in the Education of Rhode Island Women, 1730–1830.* Providence, RI: The Rhode Island Historical Society, 1983.

Ring, Betty. *Needlework: An Historical Survey.* Pittstown, NJ: Main Street Press, 1984.

Schiffer, Margaret B. *Historical Needlework of Pennsylvania.* New York, NY: Charles Scribner's Sons, 1968.

Staples, Kathleen, and Hiester, Jan. *This Have I Done: Samplers and Embroideries from Charleston and the Lowcountry.* Greenville, SC: Curious Works Press, 2001; and Charleston, SC: The Charleston Museum, 2001.

Staples, Kathleen, and Hogue, Margriet. *Samplers in the European Tradition* (folio). Greenville, SC: Curious Works Press, 2000.

Staples, Kathleen, and Tinley, Lynn. *Some Honest Worke in Hand: English Samplers From the Seventeenth Century.* (folio) Greenville, SC: Curious Works Press, 2001.

Stevens, Christine, and Rees, Mair. *Samplers: From the Welsh Folk Museum Collection.* Llandysul, Ceredigian, Wales: J.D. Lewis and Sons, Ltd., 1987.

Studebaker, Sue. *Ohio Samplers, School Girl Embroideries 1803–1850.* Warren County Historical Society, OH, 1988.

Swan, Susan B.A. *Winterthur Guide to American Needlework.* New York, NY: Crown Publishers, 1976.

Swan, Susan B. *Plain and Fancy: American Women and Their Needlework, 1700–1850.* New York, NY: Rutledge Books/Holt, Rinehart and Winston, 1977. Revised edition, South Austin, TX: Curious Works Press, 1995.

A Glossary of Terms

Berlin work: needlework stitched in wool on canvas, using very bright worsted wool. This style became fashionable in the mid 1850s and derived its name from the best patterns, which came from Berlin.

Boxer: small figure found on 17th- and early 18th-century samplers. The boxer is usually stitched standing sideways with the head turned to the front. The figure is in a walking position and carries a branch or flower. Two boxers are separated by a large flower or plant and appear to be offering their holdings as gifts.

Buttonhole stitch: closely worked embroidery stitch used to finish the cut edge of a piece of fabric, as on a buttonhole.

Canvaswork: pictorial needlework stitched with wool, or sometimes silk thread, on linen canvas. Canvaswork pictures were popular in England and America in the late 17th and early to mid 18th centuries.

Cartouche: the stitched decorative enclosure containing such pertinent information as the name of the sampler maker and sampler's date and place of origin. It can be round, oval, square, or rectangular in form.

Crenellated: in needlework, a descriptive term referring to lines stitched in a wavy or meandering pattern; found on band samplers and used to separate the motifs within a band.

Crewelwork: embroidery worked with polychrome wool yarns on linen fabric. Used for home furnishings, such as bed hangings, and for border designs on samplers.

Cutwork: an ornamental needlework technique in which some threads are first removed (cut away) from the ground fabric to create holes, and then embroidery in a buttonhole stitch is applied to create a design around the holes.

Drawnwork: an ornamental needlework technique in which some threads from the warp and weft of the ground fabric are drawn out to form patterns; on samplers, embroidery was often also applied to such work.

Eyelet stitch: embroidery technique in which stitching is applied around a small hole to produce an open-work effect.

Flame stitch: embroidery stitched in a zigzag peaked pattern; usually worked in wool and found on samplers as a border or small pattern within the piece.

Foxing: small yellowish-to-brown spots that appear on linen and paper, usually due to contact with an acidic backing.

Long stitch: an embroidery stitch used to cover several background threads with one stitch.

Needle lace: lace made with a needle (as opposed to a bobbin), following a pattern that has been drawn on paper and tacked down. The finished work was added to a sampler by cutting the linen ground away and inserting the completed needle lace.

New England laid stitch: an embroidery stitch very popular in thrifty New England. As with a long stitch, the embroiderer covers several threads at one time; unlike the long stitch, however, this stitch does not cover the back. The needle makes only a small stitch over one thread on the backside, comes back to the surface, and "lays" another stitch over several background threads.

Polychrome silks: silk embroidery thread in many colors; used to stitch multicolored sampler designs.

Pulled thread work: an embroidery technique in which several threads in the ground fabric are caught in a stitch and pulled tightly together to create a decorative hole; similar to eyelet embroidery, but made without cutting ground threads.

Putti: plural for *putto,* referring to a representation of a child, nude or in swaddling bands, used in art and architecture especially in the 15th to 17th centuries.

Queen stitch: an embroidery stitch requiring 11 passes of the needle through the same hole to make one finished stitch; used as an overall pattern for textiles and as accent areas on samplers.

Tent stitch: basic needlepoint stitch used for creating canvaswork pictures. The latter are also referred to as tent-stitch pictures.

Whitework: term referring to all of the different stitches used in creating white stitched designs on a white linen ground.

Index

Hewart, M. 24
Holland 42, 64, 70–71, 76, 78
house and figure samplers
102–103, 122–125, 140–141
household furnishings 22
house samplers 52–53, 72–73,
82–83, 86–87, 101, 104–105,
132, 133, 150–153, 162–163
houses 12–13, 35, 52–53, 57,
68–69, 100, 107, 120–121,
128, 136, 145, 146, 148–149,
151, 157, 165

Indigo blue 153
inscriptions 22–23, 28, 42–43,
45, 47, 49, 51, 53, 55, 57, 59,
63, 67–69, 71, 73, 75, 76, 78,
82–83, 85, 86–87, 90, 94–95,
97, 101, 103, 107, 110,
124–125, 127, 128, 132, 135,
138, 140–148, 150, 152–153,
157, 159, 160, 165
insects 51–52, 75, 148, 155
Irish stitch 50
Israelites 61
Ivey, Kimberly Smith 164

King Charles II 139, 154

Lacework 44–45
laid stitch 98
lettered samplers 70–71
lettering 21–22, 24–25, 48–49,
62–63, 68, 71, 75, 78, 83, 93,
94, 96, 106, 111, 113, 126,
129, 144, 151, 161, 164
linen on linen 44–45, 146–147
linens 22, 94–95
long stitch 97, 106–107
looms 42, 46, 118

Maguire, Leah—see Galligher,
Leah Bratten
Maine 118
Maine samplers 90–93; Portland
89, 92–93; Thomaston 89;
York 90, 92
man-in-tree motif 139
map samplers 58–59
marking samplers 12, 20–22, 25,
94–97, 124, 128–129, 142,
146, 160–161, 164–166
Maryland samplers 160, 162;
Baltimore 160
Massachusetts 42, 90, 118, 128,
132, 140
Massachusetts samplers 16–17,
20, 22–23, 32–33, 94–113;
Boston 23, 31, 97, 98, 112;
Boxford 98–99; Cape Cod
111; Essex 22, 95; Essex

County 98–99; Leominster
105; Marblehead 103;
Middlesex County 98,
100–102, 106–107, 140;
Newburyport 33, 112–113;
Salem 16–17; Wellfleet
110–111
medallions 62–63, 154
medallion samplers 62–63
memorial samplers 34, 66–67,
109–111
mending 64, 76
metallic thread 40, 42, 156
Middle East 40, 46, 49, 74–75
Miss Parker's School 32
monochromatic colors 16, 46,
52, 56, 58, 62–63, 72, 118,
143, 164, 166

Natural motifs 40
needlepoint 50–52, 62
The Netherlands—see Holland
New England 24, 91, 106, 108,
122, 128, 134, 150–151, 153
New Hampshire 90–91, 118
New Hampshire samplers 15,
25, 34, 114–119; Canterbury,
114–115, 119; Portsmouth
34, 119
New Jersey samplers 14, 26, 36,
132–137, 162; Burlington
County 14, 132, 134–136;
Salem County 36
New York 12, 78
New York samplers 12, 138–145;
New Rochelle 138
Noah's Ark 75
numbers 22, 51, 62, 94–95, 98,
106, 120–121, 128, 140, 153,
160

Outhouse 162
overall stitching 84, 99, 124

Parrots—see birds
pattern darning 65
peacocks 70–71
Peigas, Mistress 47
Pennsylvania 63, 64, 132, 136
Pennsylvania samplers 146–163;
Chester County 137;
Harrisburg 157; Lancaster
County 156; Pennsylvania
German 146–147; Quaker
samplers 154–155;
Philadelphia 53, 132, 136,
148–149, 156, 162, 166;
Susquehanna River Valley 156
pictorial patterns 23, 42, 54–55,
56, 92, 97, 104, 106, 120, 128,
135, 153

pictorial samplers 136–137,
144–145
pincushion design 46
pink thread 62, 93
Plummer, Elizabeth 32
polychrome silks 58, 66
polychrome wool 97
pulled thread work 44
purple thread 50

Quaker Boarding School
(Wilmington, DE) 160–161
Quakers 62–63, 136, 142–143,
146–147, 150, 154–155,
161–162
Queen Anne buildings 72
Queen stitch 35, 40, 51, 88, 91,
102, 123, 125, 132

Raised stitch 42, 45
red thread 46, 50, 73, 146
religion 24, 52, 56
remounting 18–19
restoration 13, 19
Revolutionary War 30, 90, 128
Rhode Island 128
Rhode Island samplers 35,
122–127; Newport 122;
Providence 35, 122–126
Ring, Betty 124, 162
Rue, Eliza 134

St. Paul's Cathedral 60
Sample, Isabella 157
"sampler cloth" 54
satin stitch 91
sawtooth designs 17, 97, 104,
108, 114, 116–117
schoolboys 164
schoolgirls 20, 25, 42, 52, 56–58,
61, 76, 114
schoolmistresses 12, 15, 23,
24–25, 42, 58, 63, 82, 97, 100,
121, 128–129, 137, 140, 150,
161
schools 20, 23, 54, 62, 72, 82,
104–105, 112, 120, 128, 132,
136, 142, 151, 160
Scotland 152
Scottish samplers 24–25, 68–71,
75
serpents 56–57
silk on linen 17, 20, 22–25, 28,
40–43, 45–47, 49, 51, 54–55,
58–61, 65–70, 73–79, 82–83,
85, 86–87, 89–93, 95–99,
100–101, 103, 105–117,
121–123, 125–129, 132–143,
145, 148–151, 154–157,
159–161, 163, 164–167
silk on silk 58–59

silk on silk satin 58
silk on wool 16, 21, 50–51,
53–55, 57, 60–61, 70, 74,
118–119
Solomon's Temple 60–61
Songs for Children 52
Sotheby's 12, 101, 134, 143, 161,
167
spot and band samplers 40–41
Stephens (Joan) Collection 12,
101, 134, 143, 161, 167
strawberry designs 20, 82,
84–86, 91, 95, 100, 102, 106,
114–115, 123, 125, 138,
148–149, 151

Tent stitch 50–51
textiles 22, 32, 51, 64–65, 74, 76,
78, 128, 153
themes: biblical 48, 60, 74–75,
78–79; king 49, 139;
mythological 48, 60; pastoral
48
Thomas, William 49
tombs 93
Topsfield School 99
Turkey red 153

Unfinished panels 46
United States 8, 12, 24, 44,
52–53, 56, 58, 64, 66, 76, 86,
106, 153
upholstery 50, 76

Venetian 43
Vermont samplers 128–129;
Clarendon 128–129
verse 22–23, 28, 35, 48–49,
52–55, 60–61, 66–68, 78, 82,
86, 88, 91, 92, 95, 102, 104,
106, 112, 116, 118, 120, 125,
127, 134–135, 140, 142, 150,
153, 160, 162
Victoria and Albert Museum 21
Virginia samplers 164–166

Wales 58
Washington, DC, samplers
166–167
Washington, George 66
Washington Navy Yard 166–167
Waters, Ann 113
Watson, Mrs. 51
Westtown School (Chester
County, PA) 63, 64, 136, 154,
161
white thread 93, 99, 136–137
whitework 41, 44–45
wool and silk on linen 26
wool on linen 36, 58, 70, 73, 97,
144, 152–153